D1124258

Werenfried van Straaten, O.Praem.

WHERE GOD WEEPS

Fr. Werenfried and his "hat of millions".

Werenfried van Straaten, O.Praem.

Where God Weeps

IGNATIUS PRESS   SAN FRANCISCO

Title of the German original:
Wo Gott weint
© 1969 Georg Bitter Verlag KG
Original English edition:
© 1970 Kerk in Nood / Oostpriesterhulp

Cover by Roxanne Mei Lum

With ecclesiastical approval
Revised American edition
© 1989 Aid to the Church in Need
All rights reserved
ISBN 0-89870-234-8
Library of Congress catalogue number 88-83744
Printed in the United States of America

CONTENTS

In Africa

Behind the Iron Curtain

Conclusion

PREFACE

This book cannot be introduced—it must be read. It is a modern epic with the sacred atmosphere of a breviary. I shall try to give you some idea of the author as he is seen by those who know him.

Anyone who has met Werenfried van Straaten, even though only once, will never forget his massive shape, the disarming openness of his face and the charm of his eloquent smile. His manners are endearing and are characterized by a benevolent interest and a genial simplicity. We are at once reminded of the somewhat strongly-worded nicknames that have been given him: bulldozer, force de frappe, steamroller, bacon priest. Each one of them is deserved. Werenfried (pron. *verenfreed*) was not offended when Cardinal Frings likened him to a modern Genghis Khan, appropriating everything he finds in his way. Yet I know that he has a weak spot for the honorary title of "bacon priest", not on account of his size but because this nickname reminds him of the hundreds of tons of bacon he begged for, pound by pound, for starving people after the War.

Under the outward appearance of this fighting champion, whose favorite weapon is the battering-ram, hides a Jeremiah in a velvet gown. He is one of the great criers, whose voice batters on the gates of souls and whose restless mercy can raise pity even out of hearts of stone. Everywhere, he opens his mouth to proclaim that God is hungry. The boundless misery of the whole world is weeping in him. He is the comforter of an immense multitude of sorrowing people. The afflicted people in the modern catacombs are his adopted children. He is wedded to poverty, and he relieves the distress of the poor without possessing anything. He is God's great specialist in begging; that is all he needs a hat for. On the strength of his vocation he feels himself responsible for the poor and is not afraid to descend into the underworld of the unhappy.

By his unaffectedness, his dynamism, his speech, his conviction, his faith and his enthusiasm he makes the wealthy the debtors of those who possess nothing. Rich people and those without means become his benefactors, his bankers. The great ones of the world hear in his conjuring words the echo of the Sermon on the Mount. Then purses are opened, money and goods are given, again and again and again. Full of gratitude, he pours the glass of water, of which the Gospel speaks, into the chalice of his heart and offers it to those who are thirsty.

Werenfried van Straaten is good by nature without being aware of it, and he distributes diplomas of mercy to all who have discovered in the poor the sacrament of God's presence among us.

But the chalice of God's insatiable beggar is never full enough. He wants more and more. This vagrant of the Comforter wants to console such multitudes of outcast, afflicted and hungry people that he can have no fixed dwelling-place. He has gone begging everywhere on earth. Ingenuously, he sometimes tells me in moments of filial intimacy: "I don't know myself where trust in God leaves off in me and where foolhardiness begins. And I don't want to know."

One of his colleagues recently stated: "Everything in Werenfried is great: not only his qualities but also his small faults." That is true. He is one of the breed of conventuals of whom Cardinal Döpfner said to me, during the Second Vatican Council, that it was better not to have two of them in the same Order.

The following anecdote characterizes the writer of this book and reveals a few shades of his personality:

When Werenfried was still studying theology in the Abbey of Tongerlo, it happened that the results of his Christmas examination were not too brilliant. The professor brought to his notice that the number of marks was insufficient.

"How many ought I to have?" asked Werenfried.

"Twenty out of twenty", answered the priest.

"I shall do my best."

At the next examination he had twenty marks out of twenty, but at the bottom of his work he had written: "Ten is enough—the rest can go to the poor."

On the first page of his autobiography, Werenfried writes: "When I was young I wanted to be a painter." This reminds me of the words of Léon Bloy: "The weeping of the mothers and the voiceless agony of the fathers have a power quite different from words and colors." To hear throughout his whole life complaints of ever-fresh misery and then to surprise the downtrodden, the hungry and the persecuted with the gift of love is the vocation to which Werenfried responds unceasingly.

This Premonstratensian, who believes so unshakably in his task, proclaims his message in and out of season. It does not surprise me at all if he now and then misses the plank. It cannot be taken as a failing in him if he exaggerates to reach his aim, if he does not easily give in, if he obstinately carries out his plans, if he is inflexible in his opinions, if he can barely control his impatience, if he only with difficulty suppresses his "holy" wrath, if he is an "egoist" who thinks only of others, if he is obsessed by his crusade ideas, if he sometimes gives help against the advice of others. All this can easily be forgiven him. And that is what he knows. This eternal school-boy knows also that the *turba magna*, the multitudes of co-heirs of the expulsion from earthly paradises, who, with the slowness of an unending procession, march on to the Paradise of God, will appeal for him who stilled their hunger and dried their tears, to Love, the first and last word that satisfies their souls.

Rome, All Saints, 1969

NORBERT CALMELS
Abbot General of the Order of Prémonté

INTRODUCTION

I am a priest, a religious and seldom in my abbey. For more than forty years now I have been traveling about in the countries where God weeps, or looking for people to help me dry his tears. This is a strange vocation. What led up to it is also strange and obscure. But when I look back on the past I see my life as one straight line leading through everything from God to God.

Those who know me intimately are aware of what dark parts there are in me and what a lot of things I have to regret and improve. I do my best to do so. Yet it all seems preordained: the good and bad, everything that God has given me or denied me; the helpers who have gathered around me and those who have left me or whom I have been compelled to send away; everything I have built up or what I myself or others have broken down; everything God has condoned, what he has thrust upon me, what he has abundantly granted me in his incomprehensible goodness or what I have secretly appropriated to myself; all my joy and suffering, my friendships, my worries, my holy and unholy anger, my optimism and my great faith in mankind; but also my opponents and betrayers, my crosses, fights and sins—all and everything has had its significance in my tempestuous life; everything has prepared me for the task that God has set aside for me; everything has been serviceable to the vocation I received from him, and for which I will be eternally grateful.

When I was young I wanted to become a painter. My father,

a schoolmaster of the old type, decided I should become a teacher. For years on end he gave evening lessons so that I could go to the university. There I studied classical languages but was more interested in social problems. For that reason I never got as far as being a teacher, but I did become editor of a university magazine and the co-founder of a political party, which fortunately did not live long. I landed in the nucleus of a religious movement for intra-ecclesiastical reform, a movement condemned by the Church authorities of those days as a dangerous sect. I owe a great deal to this movement, which was under the leadership of the Flemish priest Raimund van Sante. It gave me a new outlook on Christianity, one that is still modern, and a great love of Christ. But it brought me into conflict with the Dutch episcopacy, which in the 'thirties did not distinguish itself by any notable progressivism. So I soon became anticlerical. Quite a number of my friends were at odds with the Church. My two brothers, who were preparing for the priesthood, were in doubts as to my orthodoxy. I was a great worry to my family.

To everybody's amazement, God called me to the religious life in 1934, although at that very moment I was head over heels in love. The sacrifice asked of me cost me more than I can write here. If I had stopped to think about it I would probably have said no. But it is not my habit to think long about things, and I had the temerity to say yes. This has nothing to do with Christian perfection, because my daring is often greater than my strength. In spite of my holiest resolutions I have, therefore, after more than fifty years of religious life, still remained a weak and imperfect person who can boast not of his own excellence but only of God's mercy.

I decided to become a Capuchin, thinking it was required of me to devote my life to the service of the poor. The Capuchins—the only poor religious order I knew in the bourgeois-spirited Netherlands of those days—refused me on grounds of health. For three months I lived in uncertainty. Then I left the Netherlands and entered the Premonstratensian Order at Tongerlo, although in the opinion of people who were able to judge I did not seem to have any bent for liturgy, contemplation or the life of regular canons. But God judges better than people.

At the beginning of my religious life I lived so austerely that my health gave way after three years. The doctor declared me unsuitable for mission work, parish work and preaching. This was as much as to say that I ought to leave the abbey. Fortunately the abbot did not send me away. Although he knew that I sang a little too loudly and sometimes not quite true, he considered me suitable for the choir, for he had a kind, fatherly heart. In this way I was able to become a priest. After that he made me his secretary. I learned a lot from Abbot Stalmans. Once he said: "I am glad I have Werenfried, but I am also glad there is only one Werenfried."

In those days I wrote a book about the life of the white canons at Tongerlo. It was one of those poetic books with many flowers and stars such as young religious wrote in the years between the two world wars. I still love this "white life", although mine turned out to be much darker.

Then came the Second World War, with all the suffering ineradicably engraved in my memory. I was between two fires, as I could not interpret the hideous slaughter as anything else but a conflict among heathens for the things of this world. I did not wish to take sides except for love and against hate. In a country groaning under enemy occupation, I held forth that Christians are obliged to love their enemies and that it was a grave sin to deny them systematically the normal signs and expressions of brotherly love.

I had friends among the Communists and in the German army; among Quislings; in the Resistance; and among the volunteers who were fighting on the Eastern front against the Russians. This fact often got me into difficulties. For almost all who were personally engaged were convinced that their homeland, Europe, God, a New Order or all other ideals could be served only in one way: the way they themselves thought right. I was a disappointment to many when I refused to allow myself to choose sides. Very few people understood how wrong it is to require a priest to join a party and ask him to cover the whole cargo with his ecclesiastical flag. I did my best to sympathize with all those who were honest-minded, to place love above all clashes of opinion and to save what could be saved.

When the war ended, many of my friends had died in discord and dissension and lay in the mass graves or in the military cemeteries that covered the soil of ravaged Europe. Some had died in German, and some in Allied, uniforms. Others again had been gassed in Hitler's concentration camps or had died as defenseless citizens in Anglo-Saxon bombardments. Some had been executed as Resistance men, others as Quislings. Not a few of them became the victims of hard and inhuman postwar repression, of which all the wounds have still not yet healed.

Then I set up a small magazine in which from month to month I pleaded, in a lacerated world, for the restoration of love. In it I carried on a campaign against hate and for reconciliation. I set mercy above justice. I begged for love for a beaten foe. In it I took up the cause of the defenseless, the prisoners and those who had been driven from house and home, the persecuted, the poor and the oppressed. This was the beginning of my true vocation in life, to which I have tried ever since to respond to the best of my powers. The essential part of that vocation is not the distribution of bacon to displaced Germans or of Volkswagens to itinerant priests; not the building of radio-transmitters to help the illiterate in underdeveloped countries or the publication of books for the persecuted behind the Iron Curtain; not school chapels in Vietnam or charitable gifts to forced laborers in Siberia. The essential part of my vocation is this: that wherever God weeps, I have to dry his tears.*

God, of course, does not weep in heaven, where he dwells in inaccessible light and eternally enjoys his endless happiness. God weeps on earth. Ceaselessly his tears flow over the divine countenance of Jesus, who is One with the Heavenly Father and yet on

---

*See Werenfried van Straaten, *They Call Me the Bacon Priest* (Chinchester: Aid to the Church in Need, 1981).

earth lives on in the least of his people, and suffers, starves and is persecuted. The tears of the poor are his tears, because he has become one with them. And Jesus' tears are the tears of God.

Thus God weeps in all the sad, suffering and sighing people of our times. We cannot love *him* if we do not dry *their* tears. That is why I began my wanderings through the rubble areas and makeshift camps of defeated Germany, through the refugee areas of Europe and Asia, through the Communist people's republics, through feudal-Christian Latin America and through all the countries and continents where God weeps. I have written a little about these journeys in this book. I wrote it for all who have helped me to dry God's tears.

DELIVER US FROM EVIL

Before I started on my travels through the distressed areas of this world, God gave me to understand the deeper sense of evil. Without this special understanding, which I acquired during the war years in the loneliness of my monk's cell in Tongerlo, my faith would have suffered shipwreck in the ocean of misery through which I had to cruise unremittingly. After so many years I shall endeavor to recollect the thoughts that occurred to me as a young priest when wrestling with the mystery of evil.

It happened one summer evening when I was in my cell. All sound had died away. The shattering violence of war, the nerve-wracking hum of the bombers and the spiteful barking of the anti-aircraft guns had ceased. Nothing remained but a brittle silence stretched like a gossamer net from star to star over the earth and over the breathless abbey. It seemed to me as if God was working in this silence; that his hand was moving over the world and touching the deepest root of matter and of souls. A great Hand creating and healing the earth, gentle as the caressing hand of a mother.

Was this the same hand that with one grasp wrenched a thousand solar systems from the abyss of nothingness? Was it the hand that had hurled galaxies into space and had kneaded massive rocks like soft wax into shapes of wild beauty? Indeed it was the same hand—just as mighty and grand but now as careful as the hand of a nurse at a sickbed.

God is not to be understood. He himself plumps up the pillows of sick humanity. Gently he feels the sore places and supports the broken limbs. For he can hate nothing of what he has made, and he cannot despise any of the works of his hands. That is why he is always re-creating and rejuvenating the breaking earth in the silence of his eternal evening while mankind sleeps and only the silent stars are witnesses of his love.

God's hand caresses the earth. His gentle countenance is bent with care above its wounds. The eternal Bearer and Restorer of things walks through its desecrated paradise to draw good from human evil. If that were not possible he would certainly not permit the evil. He would then block for us the paths of wickedness. For who can prevail against him? Even the devil stands as a humble servant before his face and faithfully performs the part assigned to him in the drama of creation, which is being acted only for the glorification of God.

God did not create evil, for he is Love; and on the evening of each day of creation he found that everything was good. He certainly did not will evil, nor did he prevent it, not wishing to destroy the supreme benefit of human freedom—and also because even sin is serviceable in his almighty hand. He is more ingenious than we are. Every time we shatter what he has made, the pieces fall together again in a still finer mosaic in which his wisdom shines brighter than before. He allows evil to exist but he wanders through the nights of earth as a benefactor to turn it into good.

Serenely and gravely, like a child playing at the riverside, he allows streams of sorrow to flow through the hollow of his hand until they become tears of remorse and repentance. The tyrants of mankind he turns, by a slight of hand, into tools of eternal salvation. He selects them as carpenters of the world-wide cross of redemption on which his Son will hang and bleed till the end of time to draw us all to him. He blesses unfruitful hate and the diabolic, annihilating wrath of tyrants and Church-persecutors, and behold, they bring forth good fruit: joyful surrender and the gentle patience of the lambs that are permitted to follow the Lamb from eternity to eternity. Groaning human wrecks he signs with his grace, making them fellow-sufferers with his Son on Golgotha. Thus afflicted humanity will carry the laurel wreath of the Man of Sorrows to the glorious parade of the Day of Judgment.

God goes even farther—he crowns the victims of mad violence and ill-used power as martyrs and saints. His glance falls on all lonely and misunderstood people, on the downtrodden and out-casts of this earth, on the nameless bearers of the heavy universal cross who fall beneath it seven times a day and oftener. He blesses their struggle and their defeat and watches their falling so low into the abyss of abasement with a smile at their childish terror, knowing well that they will be raised again to the skies. The last will become the first, the starving he will satisfy with spiritual food and each lost life he will convert into eternal gain. And to all the grains of wheat that have fallen and died in the dark earth he will give the growth and fruitfulness of his divine Love.

Then he turns, great and mighty, to the princes of the earth and to the shameless champions of unrighteousness to whom he has given the power and the freedom to crucify his elect. He has measured their time. When the measure of their sins is full he will cast down their thrones and satiate them with torments. But their overthrow must cure them. Therefore he will wait with endless patience till he can take them like prodigal sons away from the pigs, and press them to his Father's heart, which has never ceased to love them. For even though they were the greatest of evil-doers, congenital haters and fierce opponents of his kingdom on earth, yet they served him when they tortured and killed his defenseless children because they have peopled his heaven with saints. By their hideous crimes they have involun-tarily enhanced Christ's triumph. They remain the targets of his mercy until their evil dies on the cross of their suffering and they are worthy to share the inheritance of the saints in eternal light.

But there are those who maintain the arrogant struggle against God's love till the bitter end. This is the black multitude of those doomed forever. Their evil, too, is now refashioned by God's hand, hard and strong as iron. He bends it around into a loud witness of his own divine righteousness. The gnashing of their teeth will never be silent and will proclaim eternally how right it was for God to punish them. . . .

God renews the face of the earth. He stands as a physician at humanity's bed of suffering. The misshapen work of unknowing creatures he covers with glory. Where his shining fingers lovingly caress, creation lies softly glowing. Astonished like a little boy, I understood that evening something of the mystery of evil. My Bible lay open at the text: "Behold, I will make all things new . . . ." And when God approached from the far depths of his starry sky and filled my cell with his presence, I was not afraid, knowing myself and all others borne up and safe in the palm of his hand.

In Europe

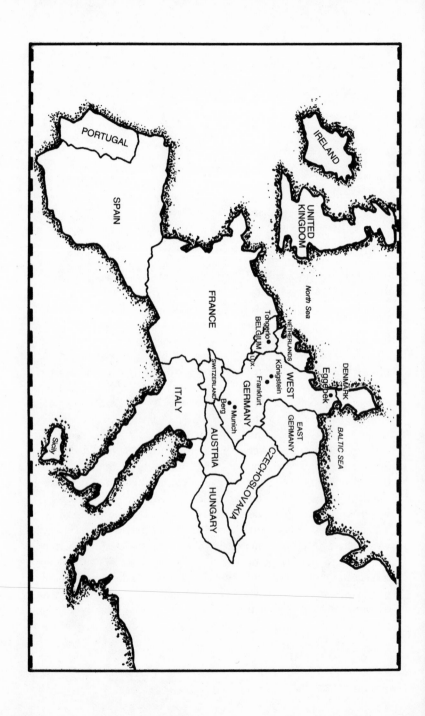

POOR LITTLE ROSEMARIE

Safe in the palm of God's hand, Sister Rosemarie has traveled the long road that has twice crossed mine. The second time I met her took place on a ferry-boat in India. There was room for a truck, two Jeeps and an unlimited number of people. The people all had to stand on one side so as to keep the vessel as much as possible in balance. After a long wait our Jeep was allowed on board. There followed a crowd of half-naked men belonging to the primitive Bhil tribe, bearded Sikhs, deformed professional beggars, gaunt-looking children and bronze-colored women in India's colorful saris, with glittering rings on their ankles and wrists and on the left slender nostril a gold pellet.

It took another quarter of an hour before a white-turbaned Sikh appeared and began to bail the water out of the hold with the aid of a gas can. That was the sign of departure, at which the whole crew was obliged to jump into the yellow-brown water to set the conveyance afloat. It was a perilous crossing. Then from the other Jeep stepped a young German nun on her way to find supplies for her orphanage. We got into conversation and she told me her name was Sister Rosemarie. When I mentioned my name she tried in vain to conceal her emotion. I promised her I would visit the orphanage the next day. It is owing to that visit that the following story has been added to this book.

3

Shortly after the war one of my friends had in the course of a journey through Germany photographed a little refugee girl in a transit camp. He had also spoken to the mother, a war-widow driven away from Breslau. The little girl was the only one of her five children to survive their expulsion from Silesia. He sent me the photo with the mother's address and asked me to do something for her. That was the time when I was collecting bacon in Flanders for starving Germans. I was so struck by the expression on the child's face that I wrote an article on it called "Poor little Rosemarie". I sent the mother a parcel of food and clothing with some chocolate and a doll for the little girl. I also added the photo and the translation of my article. I received a letter of thanks but never heard anything more of the mother and daughter until I visited the young German nun and her orphanage in India.

The orphanage proved to be a muddle of hovels and emergency sheds around a ramshackle stone house. There was also a school where, besides cooking and sewing, the children learned at least to write their names and the date of their birth. Unless they could do this, they would never be allowed to vote and would remain for the rest of their lives without civil rights. The hospital that the nuns built beside their orphanage—"God paid for it", said Sister Rosemarie—was not only for the children but for everyone. Seventeen thousand patients had been given free treatment in the course of the year 1968. As there is hardly any nursing staff the sick people's families do the nursing while their children play underneath the beds.

From Sister Rosemarie I learned the history of that enterprise of true neighborly love. When the nuns arrived there they found nine orphaned refugee children from Pakistan. Now there are more than five hundred, "but we have no time to count them every day". Yesterday five foundlings were left outside the door. Today someone brought a six-year-old girl that he had found recently and had taken home for the purpose of hiring her out. The child had fallen ill and was therefore of no use to him. So he took her to the nuns. When she has recovered she will probably be sent to the "Department for Young Housekeepers", six- to nine-year-old girls from the very poorest families. Their parents were unable to feed the children and therefore sold them—often with tears—to a child-merchant. Just to save their lives. But the long martyrdom awaiting them afterward is worse than death. Most are hired out as servants in families where they are exploited and not infrequently maltreated till they run away. From bitter necessity they take the wrong road. Many are misused by the master or son of the family. If they become pregnant they are put out into the street. Others are put to work as child prostitutes, which are very popular here owing to the superstitious conviction that venereal diseases are cured by relations with an unviolated child.

When these girls who have been destroyed in soul and body eventually arrive in the orphanage's "Department for Young Housekeepers", the nuns are faced with problems which no doctors or pedagogic methods can solve but only—and here Sister Rosemarie made a gesture in the direction of the poor-looking chapel—He . . .

She accompanied me through the shabby "pavilions" of this moving and, at the same time, horrible children's home. We passed a jet-black baby surrounded by ten jubilant toddlers: "She can drink already! She can sit up already!" they shout enthusiastically. With a smile the sister explained that this baby was left behind in a train and had been here only a week. The children adore it.

Sister Rosemarie seems to know each child personally: "That blind girl with flowers in her black hair is a Moslem. Today the Moslems observe a feastday and the other children have decorated her with flowers. She was nothing but a lump of flesh when she was carried in here. Now she is the focal point of the others' love. That is why she will live. . . . That baby was found on the beach just before the tide came in. . . . That dear little boy has two little sisters here; the mother died of starvation and the father is unknown. . . . That little curly-head is a child of leper parents. The family left him behind in a hospital where he lived for three years with the other children under the beds without being noticed. . . . This baby weighed only two pounds when she was found in a dustbin a month ago. Now she weighs five pounds. She will stay alive. . . . That very tiny one is six years old and was found playing with the corpse of her mother, who had died of starvation . . ."

And so it went on. Each child plays the chief part in his own terrible tragedy. Five hundred tragedies. And in each of them ten, thirty, even fifty others are involved. Thousands of suffering people, creatures of God, the beloved of Jesus, whose misery was revealed to me in lurid colors by the sober commentary of this young nun. Her superior told me she had been only two years in India but for miles in the surrounding country she is known as "the angel of love". Deeply moved, I went away. On my departure Sister Rosemarie asked me for my blessing and handed me an envelope. In it I found the long-forgotten photo of the little refugee girl from Breslau and the article I had sent to her mother nineteen years ago. On a card she had written that the doll and the chocolate had been for her the first proofs of God's goodness and that she owed her vocation to my article. That is why she took the name of Rosemarie when she entered the convent.

To the honor of God, who has deigned to use my poor words to make a heroine of love out of a little refugee girl, I add the old article on poor little Rosemarie.

Rosemarie, I have never met you, for I know you only from the sad photo that was sent to me. But I know that you live in a camp and that is why you look like a tiny faded flower fit only to be gathered quickly.

I, too, have been in a camp. Not as a refugee and not to live for weeks in an emergency shed. No, I was there only on a visit. To look around. To distribute cigarettes and sweets. To search in vain for a word of comfort and finally just to shake hands and leave despondent.

I tried honestly to do some good there. I gave a short

talk to the refugees. I do not know if it did any good. It certainly did not do Friedhilde any good, although I talked to her for a whole hour. Yes, I did what I could, but I was not able to convince her. She remained just as hopeless as before. The next morning she was dead, with her wrists cut. Suicide.

That was what it was like when I visited that camp. The rest I can imagine. Stealing and quarrelling. Life in the family quarters without shame, day and night. The beds one above the other, next to each other and behind each other. Beds everywhere. For boys and girls, men, women and children. Anchorless people, uprooted, stateless and without relations, dehumanized and abased to the state of growling, starving animals grabbing and devouring whatever they could claw at.

Annemarie, how old are you? Are you seven years old? That is far too young for hell. Of course the look of surprise has been quenched from your eyes, for there is nothing that has been kept from you. And you have learned about everything, without glamour, without secrecy, shamelessly and brutally.

Where is your father? Was he murdered in a fight in the camp like the fathers in the Valkalager at Nürnberg, at the rate of two a week? Or is he missing in Russia? Killed in the war? In prison in Siberia? Has he left mother? Has he died of consumption?

Heidemarie, if you had a dear, brave, strong father you would not now have to stand so utterly miserable in the porch of this wooden shed! For he would take you on his shoulders and stride away, prancing and singing, far away from here . . . to a white cottage with red tiles and blue smoke from the chimney and a snow-white bed to sleep in. . . .

And your mother? Or do you have only a grandmother? Or an old aunt? But perhaps you still have your own mother. Maybe she is crying and sick for home. Has her voice now become rough and does she swear at the men? Or did she beat you because you disturbed her behind the worn-out blanket in the corner, with her friend whom you have to call uncle?

Marie-Louise, don't be angry with her, for she is still poorer than you are. Rosemarie, Marie-Louise, Annemarie, Heidemarie, I don't even know what your name is. I just called you that because I would like to entrust all the Roses, Hildas, Annes and all the other little girls in the refugee camps to the Mother of Sorrows, the pure Virgin Mary, who knows why you are so sad. For she, too, had to fly with her child and that is why, with understanding mother-love, she loves all the children in the camp, and also you.

Holy Mary, Mother of God, pray for Rosemarie and for us, sinners, and for the wicked world fighting for spheres of influence and raw materials at the expense of these inno-cent children. And let us no longer give offense to these little ones and let us repair as best we can all the evil done, with justice and love, lest God in his righteous wrath curse us. Amen.

From Breslau to India and from Rosemarie to Rosemarie . . . thus far and still farther extends the power of love endeavoring to dry God's tears.

MOTHER OF SORROWS

Mother, how shall I dry your tears? I met you in the Congo and in Vietnam, just as I used to see you in Hong Kong and Friedland and in the dreary shelters of postwar Germany. I also met you on my way to rebellious Budapest and I found you under the flapping tent-cloth of an Arabian refugee family in Palestine.

You are not a German mother, nor a Vietnamese, nor a Chinese or a Congolese, for sorrow has no nationality. You are the Mother of Sorrows and you bear the heaviest share of humanity's cross.

You are one of the millions of hunted, abducted, persecuted and violated mothers of this century. Your husband was killed in the war or murdered, imprisoned or just missing. Your home was destroyed or confiscated. You have lost or left behind all your belongings or they were taken from you. Your village church is a ruin and your faith . . . what about your faith? Your hands have become coarsened by forced labor in the slave camps, your eyes are tired by seeing misery. Your face is engraved by the sharp edge of sorrow. Your body—or are you not one of the countless women who had to bear even that?—your body was so often the prey of victory-drunken soldiers that it has hidden itself in dark mourning-garments. Mother, all that remains to you are memories in an ocean of tears . . . and your child. Your child! The child of your love and of the husband who is no more. The child who is the only meaningful thing in your life. For this child you fought with bullies and bureaucrats. For this child you have starved. This child you snatched back from death by your indomitable energy. You carried it for hours and days on the long roads of flight and exile. You sold your last jewels for it. Your pallet, your blanket, the poor daily rations, the stolen fuel and the later gift parcels from a far country . . . these were all for your child.

This child is yours. He is your consolation, your tenderness, your anxiously guarded property, your life and your all.

Mother of sorrows, one of the millions, we cannot do much for you. Your broken life cannot be mended with a handshake, a kind word and a parcel of clothing. And our prayers are so half-hearted, our sacrifice so inadequate, our Christianity so dull that we do not consider ourselves truly able to dry your tears.

But yet we will do what we can. In you we recognize Mary, the Mother of the Lord, co-mediatrix under the bloody Cross. We want to be grateful for the burden you also bear for our sins. Through your example we will learn to bear our own sorrow for the sake of others, and we will do something for your child, in whom Jesus lives. We will deny ourselves something for your child and for all children suffering under the wickedness of mankind, to give them a little warmth and love, so that they may not grow up embittered, in hatred of God because no one revealed to them his love, lest they become children for hell.

CHILDREN FOR HELL

Before the Communists built their wall to prevent escapes from their paradise, the island of West Berlin was the last landing-place for hundreds of thousands wishing to leave the Red ship of the German Democratic Republic. When all the other holes in the Iron Curtain had been stopped up and only the way via West Berlin remained open, this city had to cope with an average of a quarter of a million refugees a year.

Whenever in the Soviet zone the screw of economic pressure or of political or religious persecution was given a turn, the stream of refugees began to flow, to swell, to burst through the rubble fields and to break like a tidal wave through the exits of the underground railway, through sewers, through windows and along the roofs of the sector boundaries into West Berlin. The refugees were evacuated by plane to the West.

The year was 1950, and I was standing on the Tempelhof airfield. Another silver bird was swooping down over Berlin, over the luxurious "society quarters" of the western sectors and over the flaunting Stalinallee, over the slums of the metropolis crying to heaven behind these deceptive side-scenes, over Elfriede, Edeltraut and Hedwig, who were waiting quite near me.

Three little refugees. They were born on the bloody escape route or in the impersonal surroundings of a transit camp. They have no father and no homeland. They know nothing of their *Heimat*—the doctor's house, the farm or the little village in the

Riesengebirge. The yellowing photo of the unknown soldier that their exhausted mother keeps in her suitcase or knapsack has no meaning for them. Their father is dead, and their homeland is the camp.

I stood on the Tempelhof airfield and watched those children. Were they not too young for hell? Yet they have just left it and are condemned to live in hell once more in the free West—the hell of the thousands of reception, transit, and permanent camps that were then the leprosy of Europe.

Three little refugees. They wore clothing from Iron Curtain Church Relief (now known as Aid to the Church in Need—ACN). But what good was that? Christ wanted us to let these children come unto him. And now they were waiting for the first airplane to hell.

Here is Elfriede! Her mother is a doctor's widow. Her husband disappeared near Stalingrad. She endured all the terrors of the Russian advance. She was raped, as were tens of thousands of other women. This little girl, the dark Russian child, was born in December 1945.

And there is Hedwig! Her father came to Wartheland in 1941 with the evacuated Volga farmers. He was driven away in 1945. He arrived in the Soviet zone in Brandenburg. Later on he was put to work in the uranium mines. Four months ago the family learned of his death.

And Edeltraut? She has no parents, their marriage having been wrecked in one of those emergency sheds where God's ten commandments can no longer be obeyed.

What wrong have these children done? I hear Jesus saying: "Let them come unto me for theirs is the kingdom of heaven". Yes, indeed, the kingdom of heaven. Soon they will begin their flight through the blue vaults of heaven. The silver bird will carry them over mountain tops of white cloud with gleaming fairy palaces and snowy valleys of blinding purity. Their noses pressed against the tiny window, they will be astonished at the glory of the sun and the clouds. Theirs is the kingdom of heaven. But they will be flying at 250 miles an hour to hell.

Children for hell. Elfriede, Hedwig and Edeltraut, three of the one or two hundred thousand. I don't know how many there were. Perhaps I shall see them again as spoiled souls, as I found Klaus in the Valkalager at Nürnberg.

I thought he was eighteen, but he was only fifteen. He was sitting quite alone in the sordid hut that served as a dwelling-place for him and 119 other refugees. He had pasted up the cracks in the wooden walls with pin-up girls and pornographic illustrations. These gave him the illusion of what, after a six-month sojourn in this hell, had been left of his ideal of life.

He had not always been like this. He came from a good family and had actually fled to the West for idealistic reasons; for when his father was condemned to forced labor in the uranium mines, he had not wanted to go to the boarding school where the children of enemies of the state were being trained to become first-class Communists. He had promised his father never to become a Communist, and for that reason he was now in the West.

It was of no benefit to Klaus that the West is still called Christian and is full of cathedrals, convents, churches and Christian schools, inhabited by millions of Christians. These facts did not lessen his misery. Should not this misery weigh like a collective guilt on the conscience of Christianity, which has done so little to receive this child in Jesus' name? Children are not received in hell.

I do not know what has happened to Klaus. Did he become a Communist after all? Or did he walk the road to despair to the very end, like the four boys—his comrades and companions in misfortune in the Valkalager—who all committed suicide in the same week? I do not know. Nor do I know what has become of Edeltraut, Hedwig and Elfriede. But I was afraid that God's judgment on myself would be annihilating if I did not do everything I could to make tangible Jesus' love for these little ones.

The spire of Antwerp's South Station stuck its gleaming weathervane playfully and festively up into the blue sky. A bright green coffee-stall leaned against the railing of the spring-fresh

public gardens, and every ten minutes Line 24 swung in a wide
arc round the gardens and rattled through Brussels Street. Number 27 in this street, a drab-looking house with three stories, was
in those days our warehouse. Very democratically, between ordinary houses and a shopwindow where grapefruit, red cabbages
and early peas succeeded each other with the rhythm of the seasons,
gaped the wide-open entrance, swallowing greedily, day in and
day out, whatever was being unloaded on to the pavement.

Passing a gas pump and a pile of sacks, you entered the
warehouse, where four floors, one above the other, groaned
under the burden of love. On the highest floor, long tables were
buried under stacks of white bags, which the quick fingers of
girl volunteers were filling. All the delights dreamed of by children—sweets and colored sugar-balls, bars of chocolate, pear-
drops, caramels, Easter-eggs in silver paper, fantastic chocolate
figures and biscuits in shining cellophane—everything sweet and
delicious had been saved up in Lent by the children of a thousand
schools and sent to this warehouse. The Lenten sacrifice of
Flemish children for the poor little brothers and sisters in the
refugee camps—for the children in hell.

Without counting the sweet-offerings of the diocese of Bruges,
which weighed 90,000 kilos and were being packed in West
Flanders, this mountain of sweets weighed 130,000 kilos. The
work was being done with love, and with lightning speed. The
sweet mass was first sorted into large bowls of 50 kilos and then
packed in bags. During the Easter days, four hundred thousand
such bags had to be filled. Each bag contained a friendly greeting
in German or some East-European language: *At the request of Aid
to the Church in Need, a child in Flanders saved these sweets instead
of eating them, so that they could bring you a little happiness. Will
you write a note back? Here is the address. . . .* Packed in cases or
in large cardboard boxes, these sweet bags were sent with the
chapel-trucks or by delivery vans to seventy-three refugee camps;
or, in smaller quantities, by mail to the knapsack priests who
had ordered them for the purpose of brightening the First Communion festivities of the refugee children.

With the help of ACN, four hundred thousand children in hell were then able to know a little joy, bring smiles to the faces of their parents. In Flanders, colorful postcards arrived with kind words of spontaneous gratitude from all parts of devastated Europe. Contacts were made, first between the children and then among the parents, the teachers, the religious, the priests of many nations. Thousands of children were invited to Belgium and experienced for the first time in their lives what it is to have a real church, a tabernacle, a bed to oneself and a normal family life.

In this way the real UN, the truly united nations, was built by these children. Their unnoticed yet honest sacrifices were able to accomplish more than statesmen and diplomats, and helped to bring about the fulfillment of Jesus' last wish—"that all may be one". Of such great value was a bag of sweets, and of such great value was the following letter of a child:

> Dear unknown Friend,
> Dietmar Seefeldt sends you greetings from Eggebek in Schleswig-Holstein. A chapel-truck came to our village and all the children got a bag of sweets. It was a great treat as we had not had anything since last Christmas. My mother is too poor; with the money she gets she can only buy bread. We are refugees from Silesia and live in a camp hut, together with my two sisters and a little brother. My father died in Russia. You gave up your sweets for us. We are poor and cannot give you anything back. But we pray for you and send you and your parents many kind greetings and ask you to write back to us. . . .

Dietmar Seefeldt got to know the warmth of the world-wide Christian family through a handful of sweets. Poor little Rosemarie fell in love with God because of a doll and a piece of chocolate. A little kindness and some talent for organization were enough to give two children some ground to stand on and a spiritual roof over their heads. What became of Elfriede, Hedwig and Edeltraut? And why was there no room for Klaus in the inn of the Christian West?

NO ROOM IN THE INN

At the time of the first Christmas day, the roads leading to
Bethlehem were crowded with people hurrying to the City of
David to have themselves written down in the census. They
worked with hands, feet and elbows to get ahead of the crowd,
knowing full well that only the first few people would have a
chance to find lodgings for the night. And as so often happens,
the rich and the powerful, those riding on horseback or on camels
or in heavy coaches, pushed ahead of the lesser people on their
donkeys and snapped up all the available rooms in the inns, so
that for Mary, who was carrying Jesus, there was no place in
the inn. She knew that her time had come. Joseph was at his
wit's end, but there was no help for it. Lonely and forgotten,
they wandered forlornly among the crowds. . . .

Nothing much has changed. There will never be room for
Christ as long as people think too much of themselves. There
is nothing wrong with our being well-off. We may be pleased
with a house or the coziness of a room with glass in the windows
to keep out the cold. We may be glad that we have all that we
want, but do we remember that Mary and Joseph in their thousands are wandering outside throughout the world, and that they
are carrying Christ, who is crying in all the refugees and outcasts,
in all whom he called the least of his children and beneath whose
misery he has concealed the glory of his form?

It is Christmas a thousand times a year, and a thousand times
Jesus is asking to be received. But a thousand times a year the
story repeats itself of the predatory crowd in Bethlehem, of the
heedless inn-keepers and the well-fed citizens in their self-suffi-
ciency. And a thousand times, doors and hearts are closed against
the bitterness of distress that is really Christ's distress.

Christ's distress? I know a refugee from Bulgaria who fled to
the West by international train, nailed in behind a hidden com-
partment in the sleeping car—his wife and four little children

along with him. He had given the children injections to make them unconscious and keep them quiet for twenty-four hours. Friends in Bulgaria had helped him, for he was carrying messages for many of them and it was supremely important that the escape should succeed. They had given him jewels and pictures to sell so that he could pay the ten thousand dollars that the sleeping-car conductor asked him to pay. The latter also wanted to fly to the West later on and required the money to start a new life. A bargain is a bargain, and he had run great risks. . . .

Ten thousand dollars! I was shown the pawn tickets with the ridiculous amounts with which this refugee had been fobbed off in return for the art treasures he had pawned. He delivered his messages. He wrote reports that were read even in the Vatican. For six months he did not think of his family but only of his obligation toward his downtrodden people. Then he had a nervous breakdown, for he could not find work and his wife needed surgery. He had rented a couple of rooms and bought some furniture on an installment plan. He could not live in the streets. Here and there he received a little support—I helped him, too— but he owed ten thousand dollars to the conductor, who was himself without money. He had to pay for his rent and his furniture every month. And his family required food, and where was he to get clothes for the winter? I know this man. He has become timid and distrustful. He has fits of despair. He is a nervous wreck and a burden to all about him. Slowly but surely he is becoming asocial. That is Christ's distress.

In the other hemisphere, things are even worse. There, in Seoul, in 1962, I visited the refugees from North Korea. Their tiny huts and the evil-smelling sheds in which they live are packed in long rows along the streets, against the hill-slopes and in the wide riverbed. There Christ's distress cries to heaven.

But heaven is invisible in the tunnel under the railway. In the semi-darkness I count fifty hovels. Not a single one is as high as my shoulders. They are built of tins, cardboard, planks, mats and sailcloth . . . and give shelter to four hundred people. Fifty families huddle here together in the mud by candlelight. They cook their meals from the discards found in garbage cans and with American egg-powder. They have to make do with a daily ration of fifteen hundred calories—two-thirds of what a man requires every day to remain healthy without working. They warm their hands above a miserable coal-fire. If fire were to break out, at least a hundred people would be killed. Even this is not a great number, for if a typhoon breaks loose above Hong Kong, more than a thousand of those living in junks on the stinking water drown. And even that is not very many if you consider that there are in Hong Kong three hundred thousand such water-dwellers.

Here, in the tunnel of Seoul, the numbers are not so many. There are at most three hundred children in this cavern. But if one of them contracts tuberculosis, they all get it. And they haven't a ray of sunlight. Instead of the smell of flowers, they have the stench of their own filth. But they do have artificial flowers. These are made with endless patience by the old women, who sell them to the Americans for a little rice. What else has an old woman to sell? Young women and girls sell themselves or are sold by others. That is Christ's distress.

I have also seen Christ's distress in Hong Kong. That was in 1962. Innumerable Chinese with no other fault than that they have been carrying out the ancient commandment to "increase and multiply" more faithfully than the Christian peoples are without even a minimum of living space. There was just as little room for newborn babies as for the new refugees streaming in their hundreds of thousands from Red China into Hong Kong. But nobody was allowed to emigrate, because the white nations have unlawfully misappropriated the empty space of the earth. There was no room in the inn. Only those who have seen the children of Asia can surmise how great God's wrath must be at this scandalous situation.

Before God, all children are equal; and the Chinese children are as dear to him as the European. He loves your children, but he loves Annie Wong, whom I met in Hong Kong, just as much. She lives with her parents in the Taiping Shan Street. Their house hangs on to a hill-slope and is not much larger than a crate to ship a car in. It can be reached by some granite steps actually leading to a villa, and if you turn off to the left halfway up you can reach the Wong dwelling along a plank. On the roof there is a broom, a pail and three pairs of shoes for which there is no room inside. The family is Catholic, and the father is a coolie. There are seven children, of whom two boys are acolytes. The youngest child is a year and a half, and Annie, fifteen years old, is a prostitute. There is no other way for her to keep from starving. It is a model family, and I think that God loves Annie Wong, who sleeps night after night with foreign sailors, more than he loves us who still think we have more right to a good life than the two thousand millions of people forced to live below the minimum of subsistence. That was Christ's distress.

There are many Annie Wongs. Quite possibly you will consider them a scandal, but woe to those who caused this scandal; and woe to us if we do not do everything to remove it. A Chinese refugee said to me with a polite smile: "You are like still waters covering a dangerous current. On the surface you show your Christianity, but underneath is your materialism which differs from Communism only in that it is suffused with much less faith." That too is Christ's distress!

The children of Asia, the starving children, the children who have died of consumption, the unborn children and the immense army of living children—all these children of Asia are the sign of our undoing. All the century-long accumulation of Christian sins and Christian neglect will end in a catastrophe. The worst is not that European culture will be destroyed but that Christianity and Christ himself will be so compromised by the sins of our fathers and by our own selfishness that it would have to be called a miracle if the proletarian peoples could ever show any appreciation of Christianity. This is once more Christ's distress.

It is easy to inveigh against the refugees and to sum up the long list of their faults. I have been working for them for years and have perhaps experienced more disappointments with them than anyone else has. But have we done everything we can to give them warmth, security, love, understanding and a little compensation for everything they have to do without?

There is a tragic text in Holy Scripture saying: "He came in unto his own and his own received him not". No room for him in the inn because "his own" have no love. And we know he is the Prince of Peace for whom the whole world is waiting and of whom we have such great need. Let us therefore practice love, which opens doors and hearts for those in whose shape he is hidden.

Millions of refugees are homesick and long for a word, a song, a glimpse of their lost homeland. They have escaped from the terror of Christ's enemies, but are in danger of falling under the lovelessness of Christians. If we do not make room for them in our inn, they will not only lose courage but also their faith in God. Through our fault and for our sakes they will hate him. Of what use then is the word he has spoken to them—the hopeful word that puts everything right:

> For so speaks the Lord God: I shall take you away from the nations, summon you from abroad and take you to your own land. I shall sprinkle you with fresh water to cleanse you from all stains. Then I will give you a new heart and infuse you with a new spirit. And I shall make you to live according to my laws and to keep closely to my commandments. Then you will dwell in the land that I have given unto your fathers. For so speaks the Lord God: as a shepherd looking round on his flocks and who sees that a part of his sheep are scattered, so will I care for my flocks. I shall bring them back from all the places to which they have been scattered. And I shall lead them back from the nations and gather them from foreign countries and lead them back to their own land.

THE RUCKSACK PRIESTS

During the years immediately following the fall of Hitler's Reich,
God's best helpers in the task of making a homeland for the
stateless were the German rucksack priests. They were the first
protégés entrusted to me by my superiors. I learned to know
them in many personal encounters and from hundreds of letters.

A mother wrote to me: "My son is a priest and has returned
from Russia seriously ill with kidney trouble. He works among
the displaced persons. In his parish, comprising eighteen villages,
there is not a single Catholic church. He says Mass in dance
halls, barns, schoolrooms and sometimes in a Protestant church.
Two years ago a priest gave him an old bicycle on which he
now visits the Catholics housed in farm lofts and in back rooms.
This is all beyond his strength. Every Sunday he celebrates four
holy Masses in different places. He teaches catechism for twenty-
eight hours a week. I am so afraid that he will not live much
longer. Can you do anything to help him? He needs a car and
also a chalice and a couple of shirts. I was keeping his books,
liturgical vestments, chalice, cassock and linen for him while he
was a prisoner of war. When we were driven away I was not
allowed to take anything with me, so that now we are quite
destitute. For the love of God I ask you not to refuse the request
of a priest's mother. My husband and my two other sons were
killed in the war. Help us as soon as you can so that the last son
that God has left to me need not succumb under his priestly
tasks. . . ."

Another letter came from Königstein, the home of the expelled
priests, where Bishop Kindermann (he was then Prelate Kindermann) supported his brethren in adversity to the best of his
abilities. It was he who confronted my abbot-general and afterward myself with the distress of the displaced persons and in
this way helped in the foundation of Aid to the Church in Need.
He wrote: "Our friend Johannes Jenke, forty-three years old,

who did parish work by bicycle in twenty-five villages, suffered heart failure on Sunday evening on his way to celebrate his fourth holy Mass, and died all alone in a ditch beside the road."

In those days I wrote the following caption to a photo: "Here you see a *Nissenhut*, a rusty tin shed of corrugated iron, such as you can find thousands of in the refugee areas. These metal monsters standing above the earth like pustules and boils serve as dwelling-places for hundreds of thousands of people. In the tin shed shown here lives a priest. The walls of his room are curved and the wind blows through the seams. This is how hundreds of priests are forced to live, in makeshift huts, in attics, in barns. One I found living in the cloakroom of a cinema. They dwell with Christ in the same tiny space. They cook their frugal meals, they wash and sleep in the presence of the Most High. Their altar is at the same time their dining-table, and they keep the Holy Sacrament in a table-drawer. They suffer from cold and hunger, but they share our gift-parcels with others even poorer than themselves."

This was the typical picture of rucksack priests in the years immediately after the dispersion. Many people think of them as priests who had fled in fear and, after a few months of care and misery, resumed their normal priestly activities. It was not as simple as all that. The words "displaced", "fled", and "expelled" conceal an abyss of suffering, violence and outrageous injustice we can no longer imagine.

Whereas after the arrival of the Soviet troops or during the orgies that everywhere accompanied liberation from an enemy yoke, slaughter and rape were the order of the day, these priests remained like good shepherds with their flocks. Thus it can be understood that the Soviets, when occupying a village or town, usually let their rage fall first of all upon the heads of the priests. From numerous reports we know that hundreds of them were shot down for defending women and girls who had sought refuge in their rectories. Often a parish priest was the only one to protect nuns, girls and even children when threatened with assault by drunken troops. Many also at the cost of their lives tried to prevent the desecration of sacred places. Frequently the Russians did not dare to murder the priest in public but first enticed him out of the rectory to a deserted spot. His mutilated corpse was then found some weeks or months later.

There were very few priests in the evacuation areas who escaped death or who were not in danger or maltreated. And these survivors, who had already drunk deeply the overflowing chalice of human suffering, remained with their flocks when the decrees of the Russian, British and American authorities at Yalta and Potsdam to expel sixteen million Germans from their century-old homelands were carried out in a most inhuman manner. Very often these priests were the sole leaders of the expelled, who were driven in endless transports to the West.

Their care to preserve their people from despair, extremism and loss of faith when they were driven like sand before the wind over the rubble deserts and diaspora areas of postwar Germany made them into rucksack priests. Priests living like the poor among the poor, in attics, barns, cellars or block-huts, traveling from village to village with a chalice, altar-stone, hosts and chasuble in their knapsacks—and when distress led multitudes to despair, saving the faith of their people. Heroes of brotherly love, self-denial and trust in God, who performed miracles in pastoral care. It is partly owing to them that the ideological advance of Communism in West Germany came to a standstill.

Rucksack priests! Their names will be inscribed in letters of gold in the history of the Church. But at the same time the hundreds of thousands of Flemish and Dutch who assisted them in the bitterest hours of their lives will be borne in mind; for the exertions of these toilers were for years assisted and supported by the love of our benefactors.

Let me now choose at random some of the piles of letters that I received from these benefactors during the first years after the war. Not infrequently they were written by people who had personally suffered severely under the injustices committed by the Germans. They are letters bearing witness in a touching manner to the love of which our people were capable.

A married couple: "We read your appeal in the newspaper and do not hesitate to send you our contribution in aid of a rucksack priest. We do this with a sincere heart notwithstanding the fact that we have been severely afflicted by the war, as we had only two boys and the youngest died in the camp at Buchenwald. He was thirty-three years old and left a wife and a three-year-old child in our care. This was a great and unforgettable sorrow to us. We discussed the matter with our son and he gave a hundred francs. Of the little which we possess we also give a hundred francs."

A young husband: "When I got married three years ago and went to live in my parents' house, I dreamed of being able to rebuild this house, which is already 200 years old, and to modernize it. I bought shares in the Reconstruction fund in the secret hope of winning a prize and being able to realize my dream. Now that I have learned from your sermon that millions of refugees are still living in bunkers and makeshift huts, I have come to the conclusion that I can still put up with my old dwelling-place. To put this into practice I am sending you the shares in question for your protégés, although my wife's brother was shot by the Germans."

A little boy: "Dear Bacon priest, my parents attended your sermon yesterday, but I am still too small as I am only seven years old. My name is Norbert and my mother told me you belong to the order of St. Norbert. We would like to send you something, too. We have saved 253 francs. This was really for a heathen child, but we shall begin again for a heathen child and make a savings box for it out of straw to look like a native's cabin."

The leader of a union of young farm-girls: "In our parish we have made a success of your ministry for German refugees with the help of our parish priest and of the cooperative dairy. Although there are only 123 farming families in our community we have collected 285 kilos of butter. The manager of the dairy had made a round sum of 300 kilos of it. We are paying in the 24,000 francs to your postal account. During the war many men

were taken away. Twelve of them did not return. My eldest
brother died in Dachau. But I am proud to be able to say that
in our village hatred of the Germans has been overcome by
Christian love."

Thanks to the innumerable deeds born of this same love we
were able to supply these rucksack priests and their scattered
flocks with thousands of tons of foodstuffs, clothing, chalices,
monstrances, liturgical vestments, books, hundreds of Volkswagens, more than a hundred churches, dozens of chapel-trucks,
seventeen convents, a seminary, centers for pastoral care, stu-
dents' homes and especially an incalculable amount of moral
support.

All this was attended by great difficulties. For in those days
when we started Aid to the Church in Need, hatred was wide-
spread and the "samaritans" were suspected of treason. In some
dioceses our action was retarded for years by the "confidential
information" that we were national-socialists or champions of
Flemish nationalism and that our relief action was inspired by
pan-Germanic motives. We left the dead to bury their dead. But
from day to day we read in our mail how our ministry was
blowing through Europe like a fresh and liberating wind; how
narrow-minded nationalism, hatred and misunderstanding were
being overcome by giving in love and receiving in gratitude;
how heroism was flourishing under the appeals of our preachers;
how disrupted Christianity had rediscovered its unity. For the
storm of love that blew through Flanders, the Netherlands and
afterward over Wallonia, France and Switzerland, also set the
Germans and, a year later, the Austrians in motion, jolted their
consciences and stimulated even in the time of starvation and
distress their desire to take an active share in Aid to the Church
in Need.

As early as 1951 I was able to hold my first German begging-
sermon in an auditorium in Cologne. After that the program
underwent a lightning growth. Not a single German bishop held
us back. Not a single parish priest refused me his pulpit. In
Munich, people threw 367,000 German marks into my beggar

hat and brought sixty-five tons of gifts to my chapel-truck. The largest collection of my life—as yet—was on that occasion. Aid to the Church in Need's bank account in Germany was receiving an average of 70,000 marks a week. The defeated Germans, who experienced our love in their direst misery, covered 30 percent of our international budget. This is a moving fact. But still more moving were the letters of gratitude we received by the thousands from Germany in the dark days after the war.

A German refugee from the Sudeten: "For two years now I have been receiving from our parish priest a share of the free gifts he receives regularly from Belgium. It began with bacon and yesterday I received a splendid pair of shoes. Although the expulsion made me as poor as a churchmouse, not being able to work on account of illness, I think it my duty to make a sacrifice, too. I have taken off my wedding ring and send it herewith. Use it if possible to help the Czechs, who drove us away, in the same way as you help us, even though your people suffered severely under the Germans. My husband starved to death in the camp at Troppau. But I shall be true to him even without a ring and bear all difficulties to the honor of God."

A rucksack priest who spent a holiday in Flanders with our help: "The visit to Flanders will remain one of the finest memories of my life. I met with so much love and understanding that I was often deeply touched. No malice, no hostility. Everywhere I was received like a brother. I was invited by numerous families. Everyone was happy to receive the rucksack priest. I am grateful to all those who made my stay possible. But my greatest thanks goes out to ACN, who initiated this work of Christian solidarity and fraternity."

A youth leader in a diaspora village served by one of the thirty-five chapel-trucks: "The memory of the blessed days of the mission in Dautzenberg causes me to write you a few words. Everything still stands clearly before our mind's eye, although the Dutch missionary-father has already left us long ago and will now have been teaching school again for some time. We know that your chapel-trucks come from a country that has undeservedly had a great deal to suffer from the Germans. This makes our gratitude all the greater. We should like the people of your country to learn that we are grateful and that they have not in vain held out a hand of friendship. It is not a meaningless word if I say that many eyes were filled with tears when the chapel-truck left. God had for a few days been tangibly in our midst. Now everything is dreary again, but we hold tight to the memory."

A priest who had been expelled from Silesia and who was "adopted" by a Flemish family: "I thankfully received your precious parcel and distributed the contents among the poorest refugees of my huge parish. But your letter gave me the greatest joy. You write to me as my mother used to do when I was still a student and afterward as a young priest. When I receive a letter from you it is just as if my own parents are writing to me."

A German student: "Dear Bacon priest, Yesterday with my last five marks I bought a book for my fiancée. I was just in time to be able to sell it again to a friend who is also engaged. In this way I can give you something for your work. I am only a poor student and often I have hardly enough to eat, though I can make do with a bottle of yoghurt and a piece of bread. Five years ago, when I lived with my parents in a camp, you visited that camp and just a week later you sent a whole truckload of clothing and shoes that were distributed by the camp chaplain. I shall never forget this and I thank you for having put the idea of charity to practical use."

A woman living alone: "In two inflations I lost all my savings. But last week I became rich and received two hundred marks for my forty years' service. In gratitude for all the love you have shown the German people I send this money to your ministry. I know of no better way of spending it."

In face of all the violent opposition I met with and in the many difficulties that I have encountered, the forgiving love of my compatriots and the grateful love of the displaced Germans were always for me the clearest proof of God's blessing. This love was for me the measure of God's influence in my work. The fact that people of the present day are capable of such love gave me not only hope for the future but the strength to extend my relief action for German rucksack priests to all parts of the world where brave men and women are putting themselves at the service of displaced, persecuted and oppressed brothers in need.

Fr. Werenfried van Straaten addressing the people from a chapel truck.

Warehouse of ACN in Tongerlo (ca. 1947–53) filled with clothing to be sent east to the German refugees after World War II.

▲ A chapel truck of ACN bringing Holy Mass to the refugees in post-war Germany. The chapel trucks carried over 5 tons of food, clothing and medicine.

▼ With the help of ACN, hundreds of thousands of children were able to know a little joy, bringing smiles to the faces of their parents.

"Traveling churches": In the first years of ACN's ministry 35 chapel trucks moved from village to village to help the people of the German diaspora come closer to God.

▲ ✝Joseph Cardinal Frings, Archbishop of Cologne, blessing the "vehicles for God" in Königstein, 1952.

▼ People bringing donations of food and clothing to a chapel truck.

"Rucksack priests"! Their names will be inscribed in letters of gold in the history of the Church.

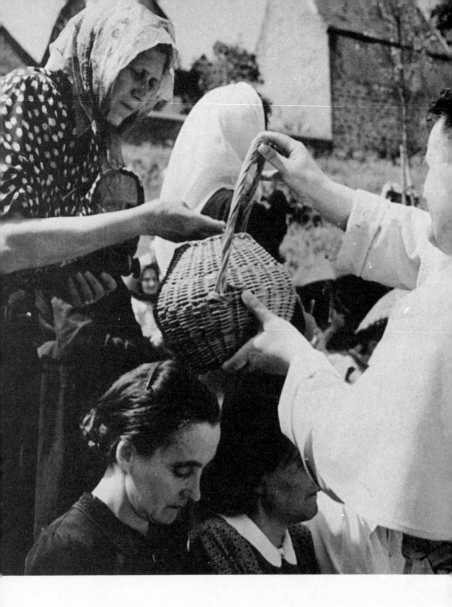

". . . ACN is a true school of love for all people of good will. People are much better than we imagine. . . . They are only waiting for the word of ignition to set their hearts aflame."

—Fr. Werenfried

In Asia

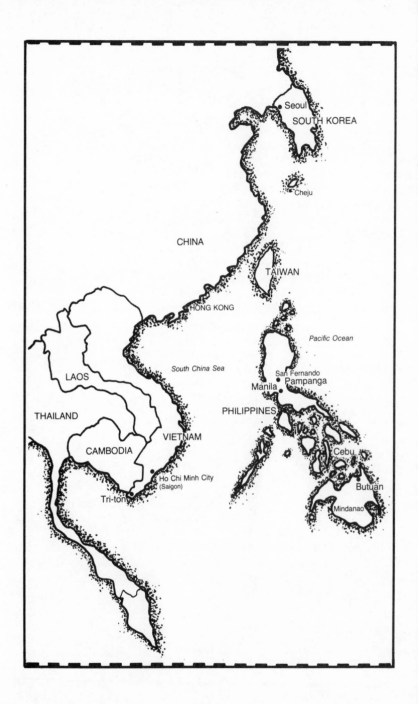

One of the bravest men I have ever met in my life is Father Poletti. I can still see him plainly before me with all the picturesque details of his personality.

It is 1962. The bay of Hong Kong lies blue and peaceful under a spring sky when we land on the New Territories, leased to England by Imperial China in 1898. We drive to the border straight across the "Area of the Fourteen Villages". When the Jeep stops, I see behind the barbed-wire barrier two trees and a tiny river. This is where the Great Empire of the Communists begins. It extends far over the western hemisphere. The barbed wire, watch-towers, dogs and the border guard are just as oppressive here as at the Iron Curtain in Europe.

Close behind the border lies the village of Lo Fong, a half-depopulated people's commune. To the left of this is the town of Shum Chun. Behind that is the gray-blue silhouette of the Nam Tau range. To the right and to the left is Communist territory. Hong Kong lies twenty miles behind us. We are surrounded on three sides by soldiers of the Red Army.

We are accompanied by Father Poletti. He is a rough and ready Italian missionary expelled by the Communists ten years ago. Now he is refugee-chaplain in Fan Ling, just behind the border. His hat and beard, his worn shirt, his khaki trousers and sinewy hands are the same color as the ground. Often he lies for hours in a ditch in wait for human game escaping to freedom in the midst of bullets and landmines. A poacher for God. He smuggles refugees into the country and supplies them with papers to prevent them from being sent back to China.

On the way he tells us of his experiences, shouting and raging as if he has to subdue a troop of man-eaters with his voice. He is a man to be afraid of. In the rectory I was sorry for his dog every time he shouted Ah-Oi, until I noticed that it was the name of his housekeeper. Even the British captain of the border guard shudders at him. But he has saved the lives of five thousand refugees! And under his rugged exterior he hides the kindness of the Good Samaritan.

He is called the gatekeeper of Red China. He found his vocation at the exit of Mao's empire. Here on this tiny piece of border and in the coastal waters round Hong Kong, everyone who can no longer bear the Red terror tries his luck. Three million have already escaped through this gate, but no one can estimate how many millions have died on the threshold to freedom.

Father Poletti knows, however, that the survivors' worst tragedy only begins in Hong Kong. As soon as they have passed the zone of death and think themselves in safety, they are stopped and driven into the arms of the grinning people's militia. The British police hunt them down. They are arrested. They are sentenced to long terms of imprisonment on the charge of "illegal immigration". Not infrequently they are officially handed over to the Red assassins.

On April 4, four boys and two girls between fourteen and nineteen years old, after having faced a storm for a hundred hours in a leaky boat, were sent back to Red China. The same fate fell to three young Chinese on April 8. On April 28 the thirty-one-year-old schoolteacher Tsai Fu-yun committed suicide when the police arrested her. She preferred to die rather than return to China. On the same day a girl, a boy and two sexagenarians threw themselves in despair into a ravine when after their escape from China they were discovered and pursued by the Hong Kong police.

Father Poletti's wrath is justified. He does what he can: one man against an army of bureaucrats. He hides the refugees, supplies them with food, clothing, medicine and papers or even keeps them in hiding if necessary. We have built a small field-hospital for his refugees at ten-yards distance from the Chinese border at Ta Kau Ling. (Father Poletti had growled contentedly when I made him that promise.)

But he cannot solve the problem, any more than the British, who in their own way are doing their best. Day and night the bulldozers are busy breaking the hills away until only an empty plain remains. Rock formations are being split up and cast into the sea. The island is expanding. Where there used to be sea and mountains there are now enormous concrete "resettlement blocks" being built, each with a letter, a number and four thousand inhabitants. But even this impressive enterprise is no solution for the problem. The concrete dwelling-silos do offer a refuge against the typhoons, but they are destroying the people. They are modern Molochs devouring the children of China.

The only solution lies in emigration on a grand scale. But this is being prevented by the nations with the stony hearts, who prefer to have their lands lie fallow than to open them to the Chinese. Are the leaders of these nations stone blind? Or are they instruments of the devil, used to spread chaos? Everyone knows that world food-production cannot keep pace with the population growth. It is urgently necessary for the undeveloped areas to be opened up and cultivated. In order to carry out this task a "peace corps" of Americans has been set up at great expense, although these, on account of their high standard of living, their need of luxury, and their fair skins are not the most suitable people to work among colored people or in the tropics. These Americans would do more productive work in the United States. But the Chinese of Hong Kong, now doomed to unemployment, are by physical constitution, diligence, frugality and capability much more suitable for such a task. For the same amount of money a Chinese peace corps could be at least seven times as large as an American peace corps—and would probably function better.

I was thinking about this when I returned with Father Poletti to his rectory. There we found a twelve-year-old Chinese boy waiting for us. His father, a Christian, had been for four years a forced laborer in Manchuria. When he returned as a broken man to his village, he had said to his sons: "Flee away from the land of our forefathers, for here you cannot remain Christians. I am too old but you must make the attempt!" The boys had carefully prepared for the risky undertaking. Each of them had procured four footballs and fastened them to his neck and waist with a belt. The eldest, who was studying to become an engineer, swam for eighteen hours and had arrived a week earlier, pale as death, at Father Poletti's house. The priest had at once found him a hiding place in Hong Kong. Now the twelve-year-old Wu had arrived and was eating rice. When I asked him if he had not been afraid of the sharks, he replied, "Better to be eaten by sharks than to live among the Communists."

The next morning I offered up holy Mass for little Wu, that he might be allowed to keep his bravery in the concrete blocks of Hong Kong until a Chinese peace corps takes ship for Australia, New Zealand and Africa to cultivate the earth and to make room in Hong Kong for Wu and all the refugee children that God has entrusted to our love. I also prayed for the gatekeeper of Red China who attacks these problems without paying any heed to human laws and does what he can.

DO WHAT YOU CAN

Imagine that we are sitting at table, ten brothers and sisters. Each of us is given a plate of soup. Suppose you and I and one other—three of the ten—eat up eight plates of soup between us and leave only two plates for the other seven. Suppose we do the same not only with the soup but with the meat, the vegetables, the bread, the milk and with everything that is put on the table for the ten of us. Unthinkable! But that is just what you and I and we all *are* doing. Because *we* belong to the elect, the 30 percent of the world population calmly using up 80 percent of the world's food production, while the other 70 percent of humanity has to be satisfied with the rest.

We are eating up the soup and the bread intended for the thirty-five million people who die of starvation every year, and we are drinking up the milk that belongs by right to the 20, 30 or even 40 percent of the babies who in some countries are fated to die in their first year of life because they have no milk. Four out of ten babies cannot live through their first year because *we* are too well off.

Perhaps you did not know this, but I have known it since my first journey through Asia, when I saw Jesus weep in the tiniest and poorest of his children.

I landed in Bombay at eleven o'clock at night. The airport is almost forty miles from the center of the city. I took a taxi and drove for an hour and a half through the sultry night across the endless brick deserts of this city. Everywhere, on the pavements, against the houses and in the porches, lie shapeless figures. I cannot see if they are asleep or are already dead. Hundreds and thousands of children in this most civilized city of India sleep and die on the paving-stones. Then our drive takes us through streets full of houses with arched windows with light breaking through. They remind me of the sides of medieval reliquaries or of the golden walls of icons in orthodox churches, where motionless saints stand thronged together in three or four rows in small glittering niches. These are no saints glittering in the light from door to door and window to window but the bronze-colored girls of Bombay, no more than children, with inscrutable eyes and melancholy faces, wrapped in gay-colored saris. They are hungry. Thousands of them are on exhibition here and sell themselves for two rupees at this hour of the night to the crowds of men passing them with appraising glances.

A little later I am standing on the balcony of my hotel room. Below me is a narrow strip of ground on which at least twenty-five children are sleeping. Some of them on a few rags but most of them on the bare ground. Gray cats and dogs move among the sleepers. There where a lighted window throws a square of light on the ground, giant rats can be seen darting and disappearing again in the darkness. I think of a letter I received from a doctor in Pakistan: "We have not succeeded in reducing the plague of rats, which is so urgently necessary because leprosy often causes loss of feeling in hands and feet so that the patients do not notice when they are being eaten by rats at night.

The one misery recalls another. I saw a little girl whose mother had died of starvation. She had lain for twenty-four hours on her dead mother's breast before she was accidentally found. She was lucky. But one of her eyes had in the meantime been eaten away by white ants. Now she has a glass eye.

A young mother lives on Pearl Street in Bombay. There is a mud pool of about two and a half acres full of hovels in which more than two thousand people and at least ten thousand rats have their abodes. During the rainy season, which lasts for four months, these people can rent a piece of canvas for twenty-four rupees to make their roofs watertight. But this young mother cannot afford the canvas. Consequently she lost two of her three babies during the monsoon. Her last baby has now also fallen ill. She has no money for a doctor or medicine. In the neighboring hospital there is a free consultation hour for the poor, but the crowds are so large that she never gets a turn. It will not be long before her third child dies.

For fourteen hours I traveled by train through Korea. Night fell, and I got a bed in the so-called sleeping-coach in which twenty-eight stretchers and hammocks were fitted up. All around me were Koreans snoring. Along the railway the faint glow could be seen of the open fires in the low huts. I knew that these huts were crowded with sleeping people who lived in this poor country. They had taken off their gay-colored clothing and lay on the straw mats covering their floors, with each other for warmth. The sick and the healthy, the leprous and the babies in arms—five, seven, even twelve persons on a few square yards of floor between clay walls and under an evil-smelling straw roof.

The train stops again. Two beds farther along, a woman tries to hush her child; my neighbor with the pointed beard turns over; the engine blows out its last steam. Outside, the engineer is running to find water and wood so that he can continue the journey, and the man who sleeps above me gets laboriously down out of his hammock. Suddenly I notice that he has no hands. He is a leper. And he is living in the midst of healthy people.

This is not everywhere the case. In the neighborhood of Saigon I saw "Precious Pearl". She was eighteen when she noticed above her right elbow a small spot. That was the beginning of leprosy. Her first reaction was to drown herself, but her hunger for life was stronger. She returned home but could not long hide her condition. The whole family avoided her. Her brother's betrothed broke off the engagement. It all came to a head in a terrible scene: Precious Pearl would have to go. She built a hut of palm leaves, but the neighbors drove her away. Then she settled down with the dead in the cemetery at the north end of Cholon, which used to be the Saigon Chinese quarter. She lives there with dozens of other lepers in the mortuary. Her appearance is horrible. Her face is gone. Instead of a mouth and eyes there are black holes. She is blind. A hoarse croaking comes from her ruined throat, and two little stumps of arms reach in my direction. Her name is Precious Pearl.

I have seen people who can move about only on hands and stumps of feet. I saw a whole leper village that was blind drunk. I have seen unrecognizable lumps of flesh, people like worms, who reminded me of the words of Isaiah: "He hath no form or comeliness; and when we shall see him there is no beauty that we should desire him, a Man of Sorrows and acquainted with grief: and we hid as it were our faces from him; he was despised and we esteemed him not. Surely he hath borne our griefs and carried our sorrows; yet we did esteem him stricken, smitten of God and afflicted. But he was wounded for our transgressions, he was bruised for our iniquities" (Is 53:2–5).

These people too are wounded for our transgressions. For they might have been saved by the few injections that can cure the disease in its initial stages. But of the twelve million lepers, only 3 or 4 percent are receiving medical treatment. And it is the same with many other diseases that in our countries have long been subdued, but still demand dozens of millions of victims in the development areas and paralyze whole nations. Never has humanity had so much knowledge, skill and means at its disposal to enable it to combat diseases as at the present time. Is it therefore not a crime that these means are employed on such a small scale?

No one can make me believe that the sometime colonial powers have done their duty. They have shamefully neglected their duty. And we are all to blame for the failure of so many heroic missionary efforts because we have deprived our missionaries' preaching of the Faith of all credibility on account of our lack of love and justice. This blame will rest like a curse upon us as long as we have not made restitution by means of the heaviest personal sacrifices for the riches we possess at the cost of the lives and health of our brethren.

And don't come along with the thousand distinctions of the moralists, with the help of which you hope to give yourself dispensation from heavy sacrifices. There is no dispensation from the divine commandments of love and justice. Those who want to obtain dispensation from the most elementary obligations in the face of hunger and distress in the world can count on the terrible judgment: "I was hungry and ye gave me not to eat. I was naked and ye clothed me not. . . . Depart from me, accursed, into everlasting fire." Léon Bloy writes somewhere: "God's indignation is clothed in rags and can barely cover her nakedness. She is barefooted and covered with blood and has shed all her tears. Where she passes she evokes such terror that the earth trembles!"

We too should tremble before God's indignation at all the sins of the rich peoples. Why are we really so well off? These afflicted people live under the same sun and under the same stars as we. On the sixth day God also created them to become lords of creation.

Where is their kingship? This is a mortal sin against nature. This is a crying outrage. And we personally share the blame for this outrage if we do not do *all* we can to help eliminate it. All that we can. It is here not a question of a gratuity; not a glass of water or a piece of bread; not a stopgap that does not solve the problem.

We must not fight the *symptoms* of distress, but the *causes*. We must finance projects to improve the economic and social conditions in these areas fundamentally. We must train persons with enough unselfishness, sanctity and knowledge to carry out the right solutions; probably solutions on a limited scale, but which can serve as models and examples of what is possibly the true solution.

This is a great undertaking that is far above our strength, yet a task to which we must set ourselves in the refugee sector and for the sake of the menaced Church. It is the problem of our times. If we do not solve it, Christianity will have failed. The salt of the earth will have lost its savor. Then we deserve to be trodden underfoot and cast away. In that case it will not matter if Mao's Chinese come and blow up our cathedrals. For Holy Church is not a collection of cultural monuments, but the living Christ, desiring to be in *our* hearts and give with *our* hands and be good in *our* love.

Only if we break at the last moment with our lukewarm past, only if we restore justice and love in the world at our own expense—not from fear of Communism, not to save our own skins, but from sincere concern for our Christian heritage entrusted to us by God—only then can we expect a better future for the Church and the world.

We cannot solve entirely the problem of the underdeveloped nations, but each of us must at least do what he can. Like the red-haired "Pig Father" McClincey, who has lost half of his stomach and whom I met during my travels on Cheju, an island in the Yellow Sea to the south of Korea. In the middle of the island rises a 6,000-foot extinct volcano. From 1947 to 1949, during the Korean War, the Communists had their headquarters here. Thirteen years later, there were still villages with only women and children, all the men having been deported or killed.

When Father McClincey arrived on the island in 1955, he found there nothing but hunger, misery and destruction, although the ground is fertile and the climate favorable. But the agricultural methods were so primitive that the islanders could not even raise cattle successfully. For the lean, black pigs there was no food other than human excrement. Starvation crouched in the cabins, and tuberculosis decimated the undernourished population, sinking ever deeper into ignorance and moral misery.

The new priest, a farmer's son from the Emerald Isle, knew that the Christian must live with his feet on the earth and his heart in heaven. But how can anyone raise his heart to heaven if he has sunk up to his neck in mud? The priest had first to lift these people out of their wretchedness, using the talents that God had given him.

He begged some money and bought a pregnant sow, housing it in the sacristy, which was too big anyway. The Cheju children were enthusiastic about the new "parishioner". Before and after catechism, which became considerably better attended, they were busy for hours cleaning the sty, washing the pig or just gazing at it lovingly.

This sow was the basic capital of Father McClincey's "pig-bank". When the first piglets were born, they were distributed among those who wanted one, to be raised along the lines laid down by the "pig priest". All breeders were united in the 4-H Club, whose members received daily training in the matter of Heart, Head, Hands and Health. If a member of the club failed in his care for the pig entrusted to him, it was taken away from him and given to another member. When the young sow in its turn became a mother, she and her whole litter remained the property of the club member, with the exception that two young piglets had to be returned to the bank. They were then staked out with other members under the same conditions. And so on and so on. The island population was, to begin with, just as distrustful as the pig priest's colleagues. But when the ecclesiastical pigs were sold for ten times the amount of the native pigs, the opposition was soon overcome.

In this way Father McClincey was able to supply pigs to hundreds of families and thus laid the basis for sound pig-breeding. In order to allow him to continue this beneficial work at a more rapid rate, Misereor—the Lenten program of the German bishops—sent him twenty good breeding sows and some boars. The results are now already noticeable. More manure is produced, which in its turn means better vegetables—with the assistance of a seed-bank—and better feed for the pigs. This produces more pigs, manure and better meadows. This again makes room for more cows, more manure and therefore more meadows. Then again more sheep and more wool, so much wool that it can be home-spun and sold. Father McClincey undertook to develop on the island, with its three hundred thousand inhabitants, a sheep-growing industry of ten to fifteen sheep per family and made great strides in that direction.

The next stage is the setting up of spinning- and weaving-plants with the purpose of supplying the twenty-eight million Koreans on the mainland. A textile school has already been built. There thirty-six girls are learning to spin, three girls are learning the art of dyeing, others are learning to weave. After they have successfully passed the course, the girls may take their spinning-wheels home. Their places will be taken by thirty-six other girls who will also be provided with new spinning-wheels. In this way a sound home industry will be built up. Eventually sheep-farmers, spinners and weavers will be united in a cooperative concern with their own purchasing and sales departments.

This missionary, who is now the "king" of Cheju and who has also obtained remarkable results in his parish work, this young "pig-priest", has stolen my heart and at the same time received a large subsidy from us. Not so much because I myself as "Bacon Priest" have had something to do with pigs, but because he has given such a good example of productive relief-work, which should be put into practice more often in such areas.

There is no use in just distributing food and clothing. The problem is not solved by a better distribution of the articles of consumption available. True relief is afforded only in the production of *new* articles for consumption! And that in the very countries where they are needed. It follows from this rule that the essential industry must be established in those countries themselves. This can be done only by an enormous effort in the field of education and technical training, by combating illiteracy, by building technical schools and universities, by teaching the nations starving for truth and science those things they need for an orderly, meaningful, modern, human and happy life in their homes, villages and communities.

The achievement of the "pig-priest" of Cheju was a practical lesson to me, freeing me from a great deal of theoretical ballast. This lesson prepared me to meet other clerical development workers who appealed for my help. One of them I met seven years later in the Philippines.

THE PHILIPPINES MENACED

The small airplane makes a sharp turn above the Pampanga guerilla area. I cannot tell whether we are falling or descending. The pilot declares that this abrupt descent is a safety measure. But the coconut palm rushing up to us seems to me just as dangerous as any snipers that might shoot at us if the landing takes too long. We narrowly escape a bamboo roof and flop down on to the grass runway just long enough to allow the machine to come to an abrupt halt before it reaches the brushwood. A colonel, some soldiers armed to the teeth and three Jeeps are awaiting us. We are the guests of the War Department in the area of the Huks.

The Filipino word *Huk* was, during World War II, the name for the Resistance people fighting against the Japanese. Now it is the dreaded title of honor of the Communist terrorists—half Mafia, half Vietcong—who are the underground authorities in Central Luzon. They receive their directives from Red China. They raise taxes, hold their own courts of law, and murder their opponents in the middle of the night. They sabotage every effort to improve the lives of the poor and are preparing an armed peasants' revolt. The inhabitants of Pampanga, who have to keep peace both with the Huks and with the legal government, are living between two fires. Hence they have become timid and reserved.

They lead hard lives. The rice-grower Constancio Cruz, whom I visited in his pile-dwelling, lives without hope, although he has his own buffalo and only four children. Half of his crops he has to hand over to the landlord, who is, alas, a great benefactor of the Church. Last year Constancio Cruz was able to keep only twenty-five sacks of rice for himself. When his children had nothing more to eat, the landlord lent him two sacks of rice. In return for these he has to give back three at the next harvest. Two years ago he was able to save his family by the sale of a calf. His emaciated buffalo calves once in four years.

If the buffalo is stolen tonight, Constancio will probably not inform the police. Even in Manila, the metropolis, 55 percent of the thefts are not reported. For the thief usually has a niece or a daughter who has intimate relations with the police. In this country the higher officials are bribed with money, and the others with half an hour's miserable love. For this reason very few thieves are arrested. Some of the peasants report the theft to the Huks. These shoot the thief down without any form of trial, and the peasant gets his buffalo back. But thenceforward he has to side with the Communists and risks being executed at the least sign of disloyalty. Could this be the reason why Jap Sagun and Rogelio Pingol were shot down on March 31, the day after my visit to Pampanga, after they had taken a sick boy to the hospital in San Fernando?

For great distances the government gave us the use of an old American transport plane. For days on end we flew zigzag across the vast country with its seven thousand islands, floating like flower baskets in the blue ocean. We flew from basket to basket to find out what was hidden beneath the flowers. At every stop there were briefings, excursions and personal encounters that yielded a pitiless exposure of the truth. Palms, sunny beaches or the white triangle of a sail at sea form the lovely and ever-varied scenery, but the misery hidden behind it is always the same.

As long as this misery is described in words or measured in figures, it can be passed by. But incarnate in people with their own names and faces, which form a living reproach, it creates unrest. Thus undernourishment may be the subject of a scientific congress. Money may even be earned by it. But the eight-year-old girl Dolores Joaquin, who looks no older than three, is merely an object of remorse or sorrow. For of Dolores, whose heart I gladdened with a handful of sweets, in a bamboo hut at Panay, it might be said that her name is Legion. She lives everywhere and even in the shadow of the millionaires' palaces, where a couple of thousand families waste 90 percent of the land's riches in riotous living. The majority of the Filipino children are so undernourished that when they reach school age they have a physical development of three-and-a-half-year-olds.

Many books and encyclicals have already been written about equitable wages. You can read them and then enter politics as a career. You can also become a Communist and exploit the people as soon as you come into power in one or other Kremlin. You can even repent and practice righteousness. But Benito Sakay, who wears a red shirt and on whose belly is a tatoo of Christ crowned with thorns, has as yet not been helped either by Communists or by encyclicals. I met him on the island of Negros in the workers' shed of a sugar plantation. He is one of the one hundred twenty beasts of burden brought together by crimps (impressment agents) and starvation to serve the planter for six months. He has left his wife and children behind on Mindanao. After toiling for six months he will take home eighty pesos (twenty dollars). The rest of the starvation wages disappear in the pockets of the crimp or behind the counter of the Sari-Sari store, where he buys his food.

Benito Sakay carries the countenance of the suffering Christ upon his belly, but also Christ's sorrow in his expression. God's sorrow over injustice committed a million times. For in this paradisiacal island state there are twenty-five million Benitos (76.1 percent of the population) belonging to families that have to live on less than five hundred dollar a year. Among these there are hundreds of thousands of families who have only half a dollar a day to live on. And the poorest families have the most children. They can remain alive only if the whole family begs or steals; or if the girls, as soon as they begin to ripen into womanhood, offer their tiny bodies for sale, as was the case in the call-girl ring that was recently discovered on Cebu. The madam was thirteen years old. The girls who worked for her were not more than nine or ten. Without exception they declared to the police that they did it because they were hungry.

Hunger serves the mighty and tames the oppressed. I saw this at Butan on the island of Mindanao, where I visited the Green Valley Sawmill. The sawmill is the property of a Chinese, Mr. So. The laborers have to work fourteen hours a day and often on Sundays. According to the law, they have a right to fourteen pesos a day. The Chinese pays four pesos (one dollar) and deducts the social security contribution, although no one is insured. The fifty-nine emaciated work people have been on strike for three weeks. The labor union supports them with rice. There is no money. Mr. So is not hungry and has plenty of time. He has all the tree-trunks dragged off to the mouth of the Agusan River. From there the lumber is sent unsawn to Japan. The Japanese pay into a foreign bank account: Mr. So will not become poor if he is expelled by the government. And the country's economy is bleeding to death. Of what help is it that besides my sacerdotal blessing I have given all my money to the strikers?

These strikers and the exploited farmers, the underpaid seasonal workers and the unemployed on all the islands, dream of Manila, the wonderful city where their problems will be solved and their tears dried. In a dream they leave their forests and plantations, their *barrios* (villages) and rice fields. A hundred and twenty thousand of them every year reach the vast bay, which is called the most beautiful harbor in the world. Then the dream is over. They are washed ashore as human flotsam and jetsam to awaken in a city with three and a half million inhabitants, where 63 percent of the families have no dwellings worthy of human beings. Perhaps they awaken in Balic-Balic, the swamp district close to Tondo, the port area. It is swarming with flies, cats and children. Here 70 percent of the population is infected with tuberculosis. The hovels are built on pilings in the mud. The streets are higher than the built-up area. They are floating streets, sixteen inches wide, and consist of rotting planks on top of water and filth.

On one of these planks I met Agapito Quijano. He owns houses and is continuously employed in collecting the rents from the ninety hovels he has built on ground that does not belong to him. The proceeds enable him to dwell in a comfortable flat—more comfortable than the flats in the neighborhood of the San Juan River. His flat is habitable as long as the river does not overflow its banks, as it does twice a year. It is inhabited by six husbands and wives, two fathers-in-law, four mothers-in-law, eleven children and a paralyzed grandfather. The grandfather is dying. I was not surprised that he was awaiting his death with as much impatience as the rest of the inmates.

There are also luxury districts: Forbes Park, San Lorenzo Village, Magellans Village and about six more. These are reservations for the .5 percent of the population who control politics and the economy. These districts are fenced in and protected by private police. Those who wish to enter must be well-dressed and show their papers at the gates. Here there are villas such as I have seen nowhere else in the world. Their inhabitants are burdened with a terrible responsibility. The hospitable landowner, who received me as if I were royalty, does not know what he is doing. His family consists of three persons. I was shown successively into a vast reception hall, a private apartment with a poker table for the master and his friends, three guest rooms with bathrooms, a nursery with a miniature bath and toilet, a courtyard surrounded by cloisters, within which was a swimming pool. With all this went four maids and two house-boys. There was a kitchen and a laundry, a study, a library, a boudoir for the lady of the house, a conjugal bedroom with two separate bathrooms, a dining room, another guest room, a bar and a few other apartments, the use of which has escaped me. All these rooms were decorated with carpets, gilded woodwork and pictures, furnished with antiques and art treasures gathered from all over the world and surrounded by a fairy-tale garden straight out of the Arabian Nights. The friend who accompanied me told me that the mistress of the house attends Mass every day. In the vestibule a candle was burning in front of a fifteenth-century image of Our Lady of Sorrows. Would the lady of the house know what Mary is weeping for?

Mary is weeping, of course, because every day she has the sorrow of Pedro de Jesus before her eyes. His house is only a hundred yards from the palace area. The fiery red cabin of a dismantled truck serves as a kitchen. Around this Pedro de Jesus has grouped a system of lean-tos and sleeping kennels built of cardboard and rags, in which he, his wife, his parents and six children are housed. Two children are still waiting in the provinces to come to Manila for a place in the sun. The ninth child was lucky and met with an early death. Pedro is unemployed. His wife, Socorro, takes in washing for the rich families behind the fence and earns four pesos a day. There is no electricity and no water. None of the children go to school. They have been living here illegally for two weeks. For thirteen years now they have been chased from one corner to another. They came to Manila in 1956 to find work.

This has been for centuries a Catholic country. The outcast Pedro de Jesus bears the name of God's Son. The lady in her dream-villa burns candles to the Holy Virgin and goes to Mass every day. The strikers of Mindanao kneel down to receive my blessing. The dying grandfather hopes for an eternal reward in heaven. The Communist Benito Sakay has an Ecce Homo on his stomach. In the pile-dwelling of Constancio Cruz, in the hovel of the undernourished girl Dolores, in the flat of the extortioner Agapito Quijano, in the dwellings of all the exploiters and in the hovels of all the oppressed there hang images of God's dear saints. And yet a second Cuba is growing here. All the conditions have been realized: unemployment, criminality, undernourishment, low wages, economic monopolies, unjust distribution of riches and land, corruption, a microscopic but all-powerful leaders' clique and an army of Red Chinese agitators invading the land along all the coasts. The only thing lacking is a Fidel Castro to unchain the revolution. As long as there is no one to do this we still have time to put our Christianity into practice at last, to hold out to each other a brotherly hand, to make the Gospel we profess a reality of deeds and thus to save the situation.

There are men with clear vision who understand the signs of the times. They have not only sound ideas but also the capacity to realize them. One of these is Father Cornelio Lagerwey. This forty-four-year-old Dutchman has in the course of fifteen years achieved remarkable things. A Missionary of the Sacred Heart, he is at the same time a pioneer who, even without academic degrees, has become one of the best authorities in the socio-pastoral field in the Philippines. From 1955 till 1959 he worked as a missionary in Central Luzon. There he made personal acquaintance with the bad conditions in the *barrios* and on the plantations. He proved to be a genius in begging, and has built a church and many chapels. In 1959 he began to beg for a seminary and acquired half a million pesos with which to build it. In 1961 he began publishing periodicals for the social and religious enlightenment of the people. In 1963 he made my acquaintance, and I helped him to set up a private printing-office in an old garage. He moved from the garage to a self-built blockhouse and thence to an empty factory building. In 1965 he set up a communication center as a bridge between theory and practice, between scientific research and concrete misery. This bridge serves to bring within reach of the common man the solutions for social and pastoral problems discovered by the experts. This communication center with film and radio studio, with two English and five Filipino periodicals in five dialects (with a total circulation of six hundred fifty thousand copies a month, editorial staff, cartoon artist, translation services, publishing house and printing office), is on a strictly commercial basis. In order to reach the poorest of the poor he established the Ang Tao Foundation (Foundation for the Man in the Street) to enable him to supply recorded tapes and film strips far below cost to radio stations, eight television channels, 1,270 provincial cinemas and a great many people of good will who are doing their best to enlighten, educate and help the people to raise themselves out of their wretchedness. In order to house his growing business reasonably well (he has now one hundred sixty helpers), he borrowed money to build an eight-story building and rented out half of it so as to be able to pay off the debt. When in 1968 he came to render an account for what he had done with the ACN subsidy, he spoke with such conviction of his work that I promised to visit him in Manila. My visit became a wild journey, chock-full of dramatic encounters and moving experiences. But the finest experience was Father Lagerwey himself: an adventurer for God, serving the Church with indomitable will-power, diplomatic talent, childlike faith, vivid imagination, stone-hard business sense, a great heart, an unbelievable sense of humor and yet with deep sacerdotal piety. I have promised him one hundred thousand dollars.

VIETNAMESE CHRISTMAS STORY

Christmas Eve 1965.

I traveled to Vietnam to celebrate the festival of peace in the midst of war. My journey began yesterday in Paris, in the cold and rain. Today, landing at Saigon, I feel the heat fall about me like a cloak. The airport is heavily guarded. There are swarms of airplanes: graceful dragonflies and vicious-looking beetles; monstrous steel insects with spikes protruding from the narrow heads like deadly stingers; bombers, transport planes, helicopters and enormous tankers with the kerosene lap-lapping in their fat interiors. The concrete pavement shakes under the roar of machines landing and taking off. The sky is riddled with jets. With treacherous rockets under their wings, they soar straight into the sky, bang a hole in the sound-barrier and disappear in the sunlight. How many people who have been promised peace are to die before the midnight Christmas truce begins?

Where is the King of Peace?

On the way to Saigon there is a roadblock. The thousands of Vietnamese who work on the airfield are being carefully searched. Not a muscle of their inscrutable faces moves. Patiently they raise their arms while the police search them for explosives. Yesterday four Americans were murdered, and new bomb attacks are feared. The whole of Saigon is in a state of alarm. What makes me think of Jerusalem? When the Wise Men from the East came to inquire for the newborn King of the Jews, King Herod was alarmed and the whole of the city with him. Here not a single Wise Man has asked for the King of Peace. The messengers of peace ignore him as if he did not exist. Herod tried to put him out of existence. The difference is not great. That is why Saigon is in the same state of alarm as Jerusalem of long ago.

The evening before Christmas.

The city is full of neurotics. On all military vehicles there are soldiers with tense expressions and cocked rifles. The public buildings bristle with barbed wire: they are guarded by countless sentinels suspiciously watching the passing stream of traffic from behind their entrenchments. The streets inhabited by ministers or generals are shut off behind steel gates. But as day begins to fade, children let up their paper kites to romp in the breeze under the mother-of-pearl sky until the sun goes down in a blaze. Then the lights shine out in the huge city. It is the evening before Christmas. Garlands of Chinese lanterns and colored paper quiver between the house-roofs. Glittering stars sway like strange flowers before the windows. Saigon, too, is expecting the Child who is to bring peace on earth.

The night of Christmas.

But peace does not come. The Vietcong have eighty-four times broken the truce they proffered themselves. In the direction of Bien Hoa, around the western suburbs of Saigon and in the marshes along the river, the Communist mortars are still hammering dull blows on the Vietnamese and American lines. Immediately afterward a tiny airplane hastily crosses the pitch-black ceiling of the night, sowing magnesium stars that remain hanging in glaring white clusters from the firmament. Suddenly it is broad daylight. The pilots perform their tasks. The song of the angels glorifying God and proclaiming peace to mankind is drowned in this Christmas night under the Saigon sky by the roar of plane engines and the thump of automatic gunfire.

No angel appeared.

But the child was born after all. Not in Bethlehem but in the refugee camp of Nam Hai on the Saigon River. There, in an old warehouse, crouches the fugitive population of a whole village. Of the two hundred and fifty-one families, one-fourth are fatherless. The husband of the Mary who brought forth her child this night was one of the sixty murdered village notables. These people's Nazareth is called Tri Tam and lies about a hundred miles away. They left their village not because of the census of the Emperor Augustus but because the Communists were taking their boys and their rice and were shooting everyone who refused to collaborate with them. They had no donkey to carry them when they were tired. Their parish priest took the place of Joseph and led them on their journey through inhospitable forests and across rivers that they had to swim. He lost ten parishioners on the way. They were killed or died of misery or were shot down by snipers. After the flight they could find no refuge except this unused warehouse with a collapsed roof, giving no protection from either sun or rain. While they were there, the hour came for Mary Thoi to become a mother. She brought forth her first-born son, wrapped him in swaddling clothes and laid him in a small cardboard box, because there was no room for them in Saigon.

Christmas morning.

There were no kings or shepherds to say to each other: Let us now go even unto Nam Hai to see what has come to pass. Only because I had an agreement to go to this refugee camp to say Mass in the open air did I happen to find Mary Thoi and the newborn child, lying in a box. The neighbors, living with two families together in "apartments" in the warehouse closed off with bamboo mats, were busy making a kind of hammock in which to lay the crying baby. What could I do otherwise than rock the child gently and press some money into Mary's hand? Then St. Joseph led me to the rectory he had rigged up for himself in a corner of the warehouse.

St. Joseph's name is Nguyen Duc Nhan.

He is fifty years old and has been a priest since 1944. When in 1954 the Communists conquered North Vietnam, he left for the south at the head of his parish, taking with him banners, church bell and images of the saints. In the corrupt and feudal country that the French left behind them after the fall of their colonial empire, he helped with the building of a better society. He was the spiritual carpenter of Tri Tam but his work was destroyed by evil men. A flood of Red propaganda, arms, partisans and political commissaries from the north swept over the country. A tyranny foreign to their way of life was forced upon the people. When his teachers were murdered, his boys who were old enough to leave school were kidnapped, the crops were confiscated and the girls were used as beasts of burden for bringing ammunition supplies from Laos, he beseeched God for help. But when a neighboring village refused to pay the imposed tribute, and the revengeful Vietcong provoked a bombardment of it by American bombers with their machine-gun fire, it was time for the angel of the Lord to urge him to flight. He arose and departed by night to Saigon with 1,530 souls. The journey was more dangerous than the flight to Egypt.

Herod was exceeding wroth.

The Vietcong, invisible but everywhere present, would not accept the escape from Tri Tam. They are trying once more to get the people who fled for a second time into their power and are threatening the life of the priest, so that he mostly wears civilian clothes and sleeps every night in a different place. For in the warehouse there are many mansions and the refugees have already built fifty temporary huts on the riverbank with the help of cardboard, flattened tins and flotsam and jetsam from the river. They gladly share their hard floors with the shepherd who is being hunted like a wild animal. They cannot do without him. Following his example, they eat only once a day. Half of their food they sell to buy planks, straw, cement, bamboo and corrugated iron sheets for repairs to the roof and for the new village they are going to build. With state aid the parish priest has been able to obtain a parcel of land. Now he is looking for money to speed up the buying of building materials. But there must first be a school for the eight hundred seventy-five children whom he has been able to snatch from the talons of the grim Herod of Hanoi. This school will also serve as their dormitory. The crowded human warehouse will then be reserved for the adults; for the scorching breath of passion and love makes it uninhabitable for children. He has not yet thought of a church. He celebrates Mass in the warehouse or in the open air. He hears confessions behind a curtain beside his bed. And Jesus Christ, the Catholic Church's first displaced person, thinks it not beneath him to dwell with him in a tin box in the midst of these outcasts.

Glory to God in the highest.

As I struggled to sing the Gloria of the first Christmas night in the din and bustle of the disorderly High Mass, it occurred to me that all our comfortable acts of homage to a God who is infinitely remote must sound like a curse in the ears of his Divine Son if we do not honor him in the poorest of his children, in whose shape he is so challengingly close to us. The Savior, once born in the city of David, is disgusted with our piety, with our streamlined liturgy and with all the "important" reforms we think indispensable for the prosperity of the kingdom of God, if we refuse to the victims of lawless aggression, to the peaceful who suffer violence, to those who are helplessly trodden down in the struggle for political power, to the parishioners of Tri Tam, to Mary Thoi's newborn baby and to all the outcasts of the world the love for which the Child in the crib has been waiting for two thousand years.

Catholic church in Da Nang, Vietnam.

The Bishop of Lao-To-Kow, Alfonso Ferroni, one of the many who suffered under the Red Chinese persecution of Christians here, shipped to Hong Kong in 1955 after three years in prison.

Three altar boys in the cathedral of Ho Chi Minh City (formerly Saigon).

Vietnam after the war.

A young Vietnamese mother nurses her infant.

Children of Vietnam.

Young man at Cho Dui church in Ho Chi Minh City.

Of the refugees from Kampuchea, many are children. ACN assistance will consist of food, medicine and other items of first necessity.

Exhaustion, fear, worry . . . and finally a glimmer of hope . . . are mirrored in the faces of these refugees from Vietnam.

A young boy in Vietnam after the war.

Christ the King in Vietnam.

In Latin America

THE FOURTH TASK

Aid to the Church in Need was born in a storm of generosity. Its motive power was love kindled in multitudes of hearts and spreading like a fire. This love was stronger than hate and worked miracles of forgiveness. It knew no bounds. For the love that comes from God and that he himself sets flowing from heart to heart as a manifestation of his goodness, shares in God's immensity and never thinks it has done enough. That is why the love of countless friends has kept our hands filled all these years in such a way that time and again—as with the multiplication of the loaves and fishes—the miracle was repeated of the twelve remaining baskets. From these baskets, which are never empty, we can not only assist the refugees but also bring consolation and confidence to the Silent Church and found dozens of seminaries and convents to prepare for the spiritual reconstruction of Eastern Europe. In this way our threefold activity—refugee relief, aid for the persecuted Church and preparation for the future—has grown spontaneously from God's love in human hearts. This holy adventure that I have been living through all these years with God and many friends removes any anxiety I might feel every time a new task is laid on my shoulders.

One such new task was assigned to me in 1962. The Italian edition of my book *They Call Me Bacon Priest* had just appeared. I sent thousands of copies to all the bishops and monsignori of the world who had studied in Rome and so, presumably, still understood some Italian. I did this in the unspoken hope of finding new benefactors in these high ecclesiastical circles. I received more begging letters than money. One cardinal wrote: "I thank you for your book. Unfortunately I am unable to help you but I have the greatest admiration for your work in the service of the refugees and of the persecuted Church. We in Latin America are not yet a persecuted Church, but we are living on the boundaries of servitude. If we should ever become part of the persecuted Church, you would have to help us, for that is your task. If you help us *now*, it will be cheaper for you!"

As this was a convincing argument and the cardinal was *simpatico*, I decided to go to Latin America. I flew for ten thousand miles, and for days I drove by Jeep through Brazil, Argentina, Chile, Peru, Bolivia, Colombia, Venezuela and Mexico to visit all these countries. I have seen the *favelas* of Rio, the *callampas* of Santiago and the gray ranchos of Caracas lying like a curse among the dream-palaces of the wealthy. I have met the slave-laborers in the tin-mines; their life-expectancy is an average of twenty-seven years, and 80 percent of their children die in the first year. I have spoken to strikers and people on the edge of starvation, to illiterates and rebels, to bishops, peasants, professors and missionaries. On the mountain above Rio de Janeiro, I saw the enormous figure of Christ looking sadly down upon his city. I visited a parish of a hundred and fifty thousand souls where the children cannot go to Communion because each of the eight successive evening Masses may last only half an hour. I saw a priest whose fingers were stiff with registering marriages; and, dead-tired after 120 baptisms, he had to send hundreds of penitents home without confession because he stands quite alone in an area of 2,500 square miles with eighty-seven thousand Christians in his care and was expected in another parish where again thousands were waiting for him. I saw a menaced Church on the edge of disaster.

This menaced Church will herself become a persecuted Church in the process of revolutionary changes that cannot be halted unless the Church herself leads the process and brings it to its culmination. The Church is the only power that can do this, but she has to settle accounts with the wealthy classes, who are defending the existing order out of self-interest, and with Communism, which needs the misery of the masses in order to come into power. The Church has therefore to fight on two fronts and to defend the face of God in a hundred thirty million starving people and seventy million illiterates, both against the right and against the left.

The Church in Latin America has to face a great deal of criticism. That continent is now passing through the same crisis that began with us a century and a half ago. The terrible conditions that existed in Europe at the beginning of the Industrial Revolution and long afterward have now faded from people's memory. But it must be with a chastened feeling of guilt that we recall what a pope once said: that the greatest scandal of the nineteenth century was that the Church then lost her hold on the masses of the poor.

The problems with which the Latin American Church is now struggling are partly of the same nature as—but of far larger dimensions than—those which the European Church was unable to solve in the nineteenth century. What gives us therefore the right to cast stones? Is it of any merit that with a headstart of a century and a half we have learned by bitter experience? The comparison with European Christianity of the pre-technical period is, as a matter of fact, in favor of Latin America. The Church there is combating the problems she is faced with, with more fervor, deeper conviction and wider generosity than did Europe a hundred and fifty years ago.

It is not true that the Latin American bishops and priests are responsible for the profound misery of their people. It would be just as fair to blame them for an earthquake. They are faced with a historical development they could not prevent and cannot stop. Their influence in the political, social and economic fields was completely wiped out in the course of a century full of dictatorships and freemason governments. But the backbone of the Church had already been broken at an earlier period by the suppression of the Jesuits and the expulsion of the other religious orders. The exodus of the Iberian bishops and missionaries at the end of the colonial era can now be better understood after the events that took place following decolonization in Africa and Asia. It was presumably inevitable but therefore no less disastrous for the Church in that continent, full of baptized Christians who are without the natural foundation for spiritual life. For the inaccessibility of these immense territories and the insurmountable distances made elementary education on a large scale impossible. Illiteracy and cultural poverty, which were the inevitable results, made it impossible for young men belonging to the popular masses to become priests. This was the cause of the chronic shortage of priests, for which the Church was not to blame. The shortage again forced the few existing priests to restrict themselves to the administering of the sacraments at the expense of preaching. This limitation gave rise to religious ignorance, moral decay, superstition, spiritism and an open door for all sects. The inner poverty of these naturally long-suffering peoples made them, moreover, defenseless against extortionate feudalism and political dictatorships. Even after the abolition of slavery they remained unfree. Up to the present day they are still being exploited by landed proprietors, planters, sugar lords, mine managers and political adventurers who keep them in hopeless bondage. This misery and the rapid population increase drive millions from the interior to the cities, where the problems are becoming desperate. La Paz, Caracas, Rio, Bogota, surrounded by lovely mountains, are like dishes and bowls full of wretchedness, zealously stirred by the Communists, into which the wealthy pour their almsgiving and corrupt senators their half-solutions. Everything is seething and boiling like a witch's cauldron. Tensions are becoming volcanic, like a crater in which the lava has reached the edge.

The Church stood in this melting-pot of the social revolution and in the midst of a development that has leaped forward a century with giant strides, as industrialization and agricultural reform attempted to slay the grim specter of hunger, disease, and death. With breath held, she watched the race between technology and the population explosion. She is a Church of sinners and ignorant people who have never had religious teaching and who seldom received the sacraments; who in their spiritual hunger just as soon betake themselves to images of saints surrounded by candle-flames as to the strange gods of black Africa; who try to find security against evil in talismans, dried llama embryos, holy water, herbs, amulets and devotion to the Holy Virgin.

But the same Church has at her service a nucleus of great bishops, heroic priests and farsighted laymen, who with matchless devotion are purposefully taking the leadership of the revolution into their own hands. In this Church I found so many glorious figures that I was deeply ashamed of the loveless criticism of her that I heard in Europe.

This Church absolutely must be helped. Not in the first place by acts of charity. Charity can be like an opium, assuaging the misery for one day, but failing to solve the problem. There is no use in giving our starving brethren a pierce of bread, which only makes their dependence worse. We must help them to stand on their own feet and lift themselves out of their deep decline, and to become inwardly free and aware of their own human dignity and of the nobility of the children of God. That is why we must assist the competent and indigenous leaders of these people in their educative task. We must not dictate European solutions, but show them ways and means, support initiative and stimulate plans to promote the spiritual maturity of these people so that they will soon be able to help themselves.

As a contribution toward this goal, we have—without diminishing our efforts for the spiritual care of refugees, for the persecuted Church and for the preparation for a better future in Eastern Europe—also given a place in our program to assist the menaced Church. This effort is quite apart from purely socio-economic development aid, for which other organizations and actions have already been set up. We are restricting ourselves to what, from the very beginning, has been our special task: aid to pastoral care. The special requirements and possibilities of this field of labor are what the tradition of Aid to the Church in Need has taught us.

Since then, we have been directing all our efforts to increase the effectiveness and working abilities of the priests in Latin America by motorization, chapel-trucks, centers for special pastoral care, the training of deacons and catechists and extension of the lay apostolate. As basic projects we have taken upon ourselves the financing of three institutes for ecclesiastical statistics, socio-religious research and pastoral research. We have placed at the disposition of the bishops' conferences the means to execute a great number of extensive and far-reaching pastoral plans. We are endeavoring to give all possible support to God's toilers in the jungles of the interior and God's heroes in the hovels of the large cities. We are organizing pastoral work at the universities, already undermined by Communism. We are trying to prevent the Latin American Church from becoming a persecuted Church. Prevention is better than cure.

When I returned from Latin America for the first time in September 1962, and for the second time in April 1966, I told my fellow-workers that we had to help not with a small amount but with millions. Some of them frowned with worry. But I thought with a smile of God's love in the hearts of my benefactors and prayed that he would increase this love.

DID THIS CHILD DIE IN VAIN?

A letter I received from a missionary reminded me again of the children of Brazil—beautiful children with dark eyes and princely names and with a natural nobility in their faces. I visited them in their dark hovels made of clay and palm-leaves along the rusty-brown roads cut by bulldozers through primeval forest.

And I met them in northeast Brazil together with their gaunt parents. Whole truckloads full of emigrants from the parched areas were fleeing from starvation and had no other possessions than a small bundle of clothes, a couple of hammocks, a dog and a parrot. It was on the 1,250-mile road from São Luis to the new capital, Brasilia. The trucks dropped off these hungry people in the dusty shrubs along the road and hurried off to fetch others.

I also saw where they came from. I flew over their poor homeland, the *seca* (drought) area, in a tiny airplane. It was a gray-green desert where it rains stars instead of water. For from the air the tops of the palm trees look like green stars that have fallen from the firmament onto the cracked earth. Endless fields of stars covering a hell instead of a heaven full of angels. I saw this hell from a safe distance, from the single-engine plane, which could take off only after the pilot had chased away four cows that were grazing on the landing strip. I know the hopeless existence of these undernourished children, and I know that they die off like flies. And yet I am shocked by the letter lying before me. The letter, from a missionary, is a horrifying report of what one of his colleagues experienced.

If you like, you can now close this book. For it is certainly not a pleasant letter to read and it is possible that you will be horrified. So close this book if you do not wish your peace of mind disturbed or if you are too egoistic to make a sacrifice. For this letter demands an answer and a sacrifice!

This is the letter:

My colleague attended the funeral of a living child whose mother had died at his birth shortly before. Almost all of the Indians were ill. They had no milk to keep the crying infant alive. Nor had the missionary priest, days away from his mission-station, anything more. He was able only to baptize the child. Then the Indians demanded their child back and laid him next to the corpse of the mother in the hole in the ground. The missionary could not prevent it.

Everyone threw earth into the grave. An Indian boy of thirteen had to tread the earth down until the child's crying stopped and the hole was filled to the top.

That is as far as the letter goes. This child actually died of hunger, but two days too soon, because the Indians knew there would not be any milk the day after tomorrow; they could not bear the nerve-wracking crying, and in their way they were merciful. In reality they buried their baby alive only because they had no food for him.

You are right to be shocked by the attendant circumstances of this death. You are shocked because you feel how horrible it is to allow such a child—who, as you imagine it, ought to be lying in a cradle covered in pink silk and fine tulle—to suffocate, alive, in the ground, crying and moving under the stamping feet. It is terrible. But it is a deed of desperation by people who do not know what else to do. And I can image that those primitive Indians meant to do good by it—that God understands and forgives them, as they had no other means to still the hunger of this innocent child.

But far worse than *how* this child died is the reason *why* he died. For to die two days earlier or later, and in one way or another, is, when all is said, secondary. The chief thing is that the child died of hunger—and this is the fate of high numbers of the children being born on earth today.

For in our vaunted twentieth century with its all-powerful technology, it is the fact that 17 percent of all children in the Third World countries are doomed to die of starvation or under-nourishment before they are five. And each of these deaths is just as bad and just as scandalous and cries just as much for revenge as in the case of this one Indian baby who was buried alive with his dead mother because it was crying for food. For each of these deaths might have been avoided if the wealthy nations—to whom we also belong—had placed their abundance, their experience and their technical knowledge in good time at the service of world distress.

But we have not done so. Unfortunately our money and our energy are being used for other things. Not for the rescue but for the total extermination of the human race. For in the atmosphere and in the depth of the oceans and in inaccessible places in far countries, death is lying in wait and the beast of destruction is ready to spring. That is what the riches of the earth are being used for, and not to provide bread for the hungry children of the Lord of Creation.

How long must this still go on? God in heaven, send now at long last a prophet who will in his wrath lay this child who was buried alive before the feet of the rulers of the earth. Send from heaven the angels of these little ones, who stand praying before your countenance, and let them lay the corpses of the starving in the houses of the rulers until they scream with horror and come to repentance. And if they will not repent, O God, chastise them before it is too late. Send your archangel Michael, the prince of your heavenly hosts, to defend these innocent children against the wickedness of your enemies. For your enemies are those who do not appease hunger but invest the money in arsenals of destruction and thus force others to do the same.

But perhaps God, who is a God of patience, is waiting for us. Perhaps he is resigned to the bad will or blindness of the mighty of this earth because he has not destined them to solve the problem of hunger and disease. Perhaps he has reserved this task for his Church, which has been commanded to preach the love of the Lord and to demonstrate it. That is part of her message. Just as Christ himself went around doing good, feeding the hungry and healing the sick, so the Church should relieve human need. Her preaching of salvation would not be credible and would become merely academic if she did not stress her gospel of love by practical help. And if God really intends to restore everything and once more combine and reunite everything under the one Head which is Christ, how greatly would not this grand plan be served if *we*, in Christ's name, were to solve the world problem of hunger.

We are faced by the fact that secular authorities either neglect

their duties or make such huge mistakes that the aim in view is
not attained. Why should we not achieve it ourselves? Why
cannot Christianity become so ready to make sacrifices that the
Church would really be able to give examples and to show
models for the solution of this problem? For you should not
think that this problem cannot be solved! There was a time when
people starved without anyone being able to do anything about
it. It was then a kind of natural catastrophe against which men
were powerless. Or maybe nothing was known about it: there
was no one in the civilized world who had ever heard about it.
Or if it was known, the difficulties were so unsurpassably great
that only a few saints could feel themselves called to extend a
helping hand. Father Damian was one of these. A man to be
admired—but who could follow his example? There has never
been a pope able or willing to require so much heroism from
the Christian people. The problem was insoluble, and hence
there was no obligation to undertake such an extraordinary enterprise.

But now the circumstances are quite different. Such things
need not happen again. This is no earthquake or flood that we
are unable to control. This is quite simply a sin of omission for
each one of us who does not at least partially set apart his superfluous earnings or superfluous possessions to make the solution
of this problem possible. This problem can certainly be solved.
Not with a little charity, but with just so much means as the
poor nations need to raise themselves out of their wretchedness.
For their misery is not a result of hunger; rather their hunger is
caused by their inward poverty. It is owing to their lack of
training and culture that they have become degraded to second-
class people who do not possess the freedom of the children of
God and do not reflect God's countenance. Thus they have remained dependent on nature and on tyrants and bloodsuckers.
The solution therefore does not begin with charity, which can
alleviate for one day the pain of their misery but makes their
dependence worse. The solution begins with elementary education.

The Brazilian Ministry of Education estimates that of the

hundred forty million Brazilians, fifty million are illiterate. Seventy percent of the children who do not attend school live in the northeast. And we have a worldwide population explosion that by the year 2025 will bring the world population up to eight billion. In itself, this is not disquieting, as the earth can feed two hundred billion. But this is impossible as long as millions of undertrained farmers still go on working their fields with crooked cudgels and wooden diggers. In this case, production will remain far below the demand: that is the reason why the Brazilian farmer produces only 5 percent of what the Canadian farmer produces. For one Canadian, twenty Brazilians have to work hard to obtain the same result. Not because the Brazilian is indolent but because he has no technical implements. Technology must therefore keep pace with the population explosion, and education is the only way to make this progress possible.

Illiterate people cannot be sent to agricultural schools or be trained as engineers! Without engineers there can, however, be no factories. Without factories, no agricultural machines and no fertilizers. Without the latter, no proper harvest, no prosperity, no food. Without food, no calories, no health, no resistance to disease and no strength to work. Without energy, still worse harvests, still less food and so still less energy! And so things go on. The one necessity invokes another till we have a vicious circle of misery, a whirlpool of destruction in which these people are being irresistibly drawn down to utter destruction unless we, outsiders, intervene by providing education. There is no need for alarm. Do not have in mind our own complicated system of education with its enormous investments and expensive staff. These are of no use in the development areas. That would be throwing money away. Things have to be quite different there. Like this, for instance:

In northeast Brazil, I visited Natal. It is a diocese with one million one hundred thousand Catholics and sixty priests. In spite of the shortage of priests, it is one of the more flourishing dioceses in the world! The then-ruling bishop, Don Eugenio de Araujo Sales, stopped the building of a cathedral started by his predecessor. The scaffolding around the half-completed pillars had collapsed. Birds had built their nests in the concrete window-frames. Fragments of walls were covered with grass and weeds. It looked pitiful, yet it was splendid. For this young bishop did not desire a stone cathedral; he wanted a living church. With the money allocated for the cathedral he bought a radio-transmitter for educational purposes, for which the current expenses were covered by commercial advertising. The lessons are given by a team of thirty-nine persons, some salaried, some volunteers—an apostolically inspired staff whose leader was the bishop himself. The curriculum includes not only reading and writing and religion, but also modern agricultural methods and everything that illiterate people require to raise themselves from misery.

In the interior more than fifteen hundred radio schools have been set up. The whole school consists of a transistor apparatus costing twenty dollars and tuned in to the transmitter in Natal. The rest costs nothing. In most places the receiver is set up in a cabin that can be used gratis for a few hours every evening.

I have visited such a school. Seventeen pupils, ages six to sixty, sat around a wooden table. A twenty-year-old lad, with his tongue between his teeth, was learning to write the difficult letter F. Beside the radio stood the *monitora*, a volunteer who knew a little more than the others, armed with a piece of chalk and a blackboard. She had taken a course and serves as the liaison between the teacher at the transmitter and this class in the interior. On the wall hung three kerosene lamps. Overhead was the tiled roof. Next door, a baby was crying. The *monitora* is the lady of the house. Her husband is a bricklayer. She is twenty-nine years old and is expecting her eleventh child (six have died). Her name is Maria Anita de Mello. Her eldest daughter helps to distribute the lesson books. Her school has three courses, with forty-three pupils in all. I read a few posters on the wall: "More hygiene, less disease . . . Clean your teeth . . . Don't spit". Every week the pupils pay one egg, for as a matter of principle they get nothing for nothing. The eggs are sold in the village, and the proceeds help pay for the lesson books.

In this way, with courage, imagination and the Holy Spirit, a problem can be attacked. A school for twenty dollars! A source of blessing but also a source of grace! For every Sunday evening at five o'clock the bishop's Mass is broadcast over the radio. And in more than fifteen hundred radio schools his isolated flock are gathered around the radio set. Most of them only very seldom in their lives enjoy the consolation of a priest. But Sunday after Sunday they celebrate the Eucharist together with their chief shepherd and listen to the short sermon he preaches to them. He is a bishop without a cathedral, but every week he is a priest, a father and a teacher for at least sixty thousand poor, ignorant, hungry Christians who gratefully honor him because he is helping them to rise from their misery.

Let me end this story with the beginning; with the little Indian baby who was buried alive with his dead mother. He was a nameless child, but was baptized and is with God. And God has sent him to you to knock on your heart and on your conscience with his tiny fingers. Is your heart still good and your conscience still sensitive?

We all have something to make up for because we all have fallen short in love and care for our poor brothers of whom we so seldom think. A radio school costs twenty dollars. What can *you* do? What can your family do? What can your firm do? If all of you together can collect the money for twenty thousand radio schools, a million poor people will be given a chance to rise up out of their wretchedness. Then this Indian baby will not have died in vain.

MEDITATIONS IN THE NIGHT

It is nighttime in Pindaré Mirim. Palms like ostrich-feathers are waving in the firmament, and a sultry wind shuffles whisperings through the frayed leaves. Far away in the forest there is the rattle of a drum. There natives are dancing the *butacada* while drinking cane-sugar gin. It is a nocturnal orgy, a survival from the time when the planters organized excesses to excite the sexual energy of the exhausted slaves so as to keep up the numbers of their human stock. After the abolition of slavery, the wretchedness of the people remained so grave that in the old slave centers of Bahia, Rio Grande do Norte and Maranhão the narcotic stimulus of the *butacada* still continued to be the only consolation of the poor.

I cannot sleep. Let me slip out of my hammock and look at the stars, which are so much clearer here than in the cloudy skies of northwest Europe.

It has been an exhausting day. In a Jeep, accompanied by the archbishop of São Luis and two German Franciscans, I crossed this northeast Brazilian territory of red clay and green forests. Half a million refugees from the hell of the *seca*—the parching drought—have settled here along the road-under-construction leading straight through the virgin forest to the new capital, Brasilia.

The road is not yet completed but passable. Our Jeep rocks like a ship in a hurricane. We bump along for a whole hour in the wake of a lurching column of trucks that are not to be overtaken. It is bright daylight, but the oncoming traffic looms with flaring headlights out of the ocher-colored cloud that surrounds us like a thunderstorm. The bushes are covered with a rusty-brown dust. Withered-looking huts of clay and palm leaves squat in the grass. Half a million emigrants are huddled together along this red pathway that creeps slowly southward.

This is where our Charity is building a new fortress for God, with churches, rectories and a school for catechists, together with Jeeps and chapel-trucks that will drive continually up and down the tediously straight road to visit God's deserted flocks.

Hitherto, parish work has been very laboriously undertaken by the German Franciscans, who have a religious house at Bacabal, and by the forty-year-old parish priest of Pindaré Mirim, who is our host. His name is Father Francisco das Chagas

Vasconcello. He serves four churches and forty-five chapels attended by eighty thousand inhabitants scattered over an extensive area of 6,875 square miles. He covers 4,500 miles on horseback every year, and in the preceding three weeks he baptized 999 children and solemnized 105 marriages. His parish is 125 miles from end to end; and in six years' time he has covered about 100 miles of it. A large remote section he cannot reach on horseback. No priest has ever been there.

When I promised him a Jeep and a church at the expense of my benefactors, the padre shrugged his shoulders incredulously. I don't know which he doubted more, me or my benefactors. But the archbishop, who had already experienced that generosity, overcame his mistrust. After that he began to smile; and now he is snoring contentedly in his hammock next to mine and the archbishop's, under the veranda of his humble rectory.

Father Celsus in Bacabal also smiled the day before yesterday when I asked him if he would take me to visit his chapels. He is a German Franciscan, thin as a rail and forty-three years old, who after four years at the front, five wounds, two years as a prisoner of war and a little bit of theology, was ordained in 1949. He is now the pastor of an extensive area—two parishes consisting of two hundred fifty villages with a total of a hundred and twenty-five thousand souls. He serves two churches and eighty-three chapels, which he visits at least once a year.

We traveled over trackless country, followed by a swarm of photographers, peddlers, bakers, fortune-tellers and conjurers on donkeys and horses. For the *desobriga*, the day on which a village performs its Easter duties is at the same time fair- and market-day. More than two thousand people from the whole neighborhood, gathered together around the church, welcomed us with blunderbusses and cheers.

They brought us a gas can full of muddy water. We took off our hats and with the aid of a tin can poured the precious liquid over our hot and dusty heads. Then Father Celsus disappeared into the confessional. Those who had confessed three months ago he would not receive; the others had priority. He heard confessions for eight hours, till late in the night. Then we strung up our hammocks in the sacristy. We had a short, quick sleep. When I awakened, at six o'clock, the padre was once more in the confessional—till ten o'clock. Then he said Mass and gave his annual sermon; and the two of us gave Holy Communion.

He took his breakfast in the sacristy at eleven o'clock. It was stiflingly hot there. During breakfast he began to register the baptisms; there were 117. With an average of forty baptisms an hour, he wrote till five minutes to two. His fingers were stiff, and the sweat was pouring down his face. I could not help him, because I knew no Portuguese.

When all the candidates for baptism, with fathers and mothers, godfathers and godmothers, birthplaces and particulars had been registered in long columns, Holy Matrimony was given a turn. Twenty-seven couples presented themselves, often complete with a baby. Who in this tropical climate would dare demand that they wait with love till a priest is available to solemnize the marriage? Nevertheless marriage is a serious matter requiring examination, instruction and bookkeeping. So once more the priest attends to his registers. At four o'clock he has finished his administrative work. Then he begins to baptize. In this I can help him. Seven rows of proud mothers with yelling infants take their places in the chapel. One row waits outside in the shade. After the baptisms, in the smoky light of kerosene lamps, come the marriages. At eight o'clock in the evening everything is finished. But here work is never done. Two hundred people, waiting from the previous evening, are besieging the confessional. I glance at Father Celsus' weary face. He shrugs his shoulders and addresses his people for the last time, sending them away with nothing but the cold comfort of "next year perhaps". For he cannot possibly stay. He is hours overdue. Twelve miles farther on, fifteen hundred other parishioners are awaiting his arrival. Two hundred well-intentioned sinners, closer to the Church of the Poor than over-fed Europe, have to return unconfessed and unconsoled to their lonely cabins. They are ignorant and do not believe in the power of a general absolution. They desire to confess their sins and unburden their hearts to the padre. Some had come from seventy miles away.

Father Celsus presses my hand dejectedly as he turns his horse, like a thin specter in the night, in the direction of the next chapel. He hears thirteen thousand confessions a year. This is the third part of what is necessary to allow everyone to do his Easter duties. In the waiting Jeep I return to Bacabal with anger in my heart, for I know that this state of affairs is not God's will.

If it is true that Christ instituted the priesthood so that he could always be with the poor, something must be changed in the Church. We must all of us ask ourselves how God's gift, never absent in the Church, can be distributed in a better way. We must not consider any sacrifice too severe if we are to help Celsus and his colleagues.

That night at Pindaré Mirim, I longed fervently to stay with Celsus. Under the stars and waving palms I laid stout plans for God's fortress in the district of Bacabal. I prayed for priests, and for money. And while I prayed I had you in mind. . . .

MONSIGNOR AT THE FRONT

It was 1962. As the Jeep stopped in the center of the village, an untidy-looking monsignor ran to meet us. This had to be the famous priest of São Paulo do Potengi. He was forty-five years old, and his name was Monsignor Expedito Sobral de Medeiros. A few violet-colored buttons dangled from his unbuttoned cassock, whose purple pipings had been bleached by the sun. This threadbare ceremonial garment must in its time have arrayed many high dignitaries before it strayed to this sector of the Church at the front together with the title of monsignor.

Monsignor Expedito is small, slight and thin as a lath. Above his large aquiline nose, his spectacles were pushed up onto his forehead. Prominent cheekbones, large ears, a beard a quarter-of-an-inch long and a wide mouth with ill-fitting dentures form the most characteristic features of his remarkable appearance.

This is the man who in the span of nineteen years baptized twenty-eight thousand children. His parish covers an area of 750 square miles and contains one church, nineteen chapels and thirty-one thousand souls. On Sunday he celebrates three Masses in his parish church, which is no more than a rough shell. In this diocese of a bishop without a cathedral, the parish priests too are of the opinion that God has no pleasure in luxurious churches as long as his divine life is choked with misery in the hearts of the faithful.

Monsignor Expedito visits six of his chapels every month; the remaining thirteen receive a visit three times a year. For the last five years he has had a Jeep; but for fourteen years he traversed his parish on horseback, celebrating Mass in chapels and remote farms, preaching, baptizing, hearing confessions. In his territory he established a hundred and fifty radio schools, a secondary school, a maternity home and a series of kindergartens. He organized not only a religious revival but also adult education, the pooling of common interests, cooperative stores, wholesome forms of sport and recreation, modern agricultural instruction, press, radio, and health centers.

He is one of the founders of the Natal movement, which, in this largest underdeveloped area of the Western Hemisphere, is furthering social reform under the driving power of the Church as an expression of Christian love that desires happiness for all men.

Northeast Brazil is three times as large as France and has forty-one million inhabitants. According to a Brazilian survey in 1986, only 58.7 percent of school-age children in rural areas attend school. The average annual income per capita is below a hundred dollars. Seventy percent of the children who do not attend school live in the northeast. Nearly the whole of the interior is part of the notorious drought area. The lack of rain not infrequently becomes a national disaster. In the years 1953 and 1958, there was no harvest. The cattle had to be slaughtered. Thousands and thousands of families died of hunger and thirst; and millions tried to save their lives by desperate flight in all directions. In the less arid years, the inhabitants strive to earn a livelihood with cattle-farming and cotton growing. The farms and the miserable livestock are the property of the landowners. The tenants are allowed to sell half of the cotton crop for their own benefit, but this income is not enough to live on.

The fertile coastal area produces sugar cane, but owing to a merciless capitalist system that exhausts the ground by overplanting and robs the people, the latter are worse off than in times of slavery, when the planters out of sheer self-interest had a little care for their human livestock.

The poverty of the drought areas and the capitalist exploitation of the fertile areas drive millions to the urban centers, where they are huddled together in overwhelming numbers in uninhabitable hovels, an unemployed subproletariat living by theft, beggary and prostitution.

In this deadly, menacing area, God's spirit roused up a movement that is spreading like wildfire throughout the whole of Brazil; and the dynamism, talent for improvisation and incomparable self-abnegation of its leaders and workers have won the unlimited confidence of the downtrodden people, who are now being educated by the Church to the consciousness of their natural and supernatural dignity. The movement arose in Natal under the leadership of the then young bishop of Natal, Dom Eugenio de Aranjo Sales, who, an hour after I left the airplane, rushed me by Jeep along the rust-brown roads of Rio Grande do Norte to the model parish of São Paulo do Potengi.

In this parish most of the plans conceived in Natal are being tried out. This experimental station for social Christianity is run by the exotic Monsignor Expedito, whom I have described above. He is a genius in the art of transposing all theories into workable practice. He is able so intelligently and good-humoredly to make these prototypes acceptable so that they can be applied a thousandfold throughout the whole of northeast Brazil.

Monsignor Expedito laughs from ear to ear, and, widely

gesticulating and speaking in broken French, drives us to his rectory. Dozens of parishioners follow. They sit in his chairs and drink his coffee, and they pop in and out as if they lived there. "My rectory is the home of the parish", he explains, while his flock standing around the table watch us eat. Then he tells us of his parish work and social action. He is not fighting Communism but the misery that effaces God's features from the human countenance and destroys the image of the Lord of Creation. In his flowery language he replies to my questions, tells of his experiences, describes the battles he has victoriously fought.

With the greatest simplicity he sums up the order of the day for his chapel visits: four hours of confession; two hours for Mass celebration, preaching, distribution of Communion and teaching; half an hour for food; two hours meeting with social-action workers; two hours visiting of the sick and dying; one hour for a lecture with slides; and one hour traveling to the next chapel, where he takes supper at nine o'clock before hanging up his hammock for the night.

Under the burning noonday sun he conducts us through the village and shows us on the door of the maternity home the list of families that have taken upon themselves to care for a young mother. Four families per bed, who take turns to bring a dish of food to a poor woman from the interior who is having her baby here: Mona Gomes Soccorro Guilher, Josefa Pimentel, Didi Araujo . . . simple housewives who have understood more of Christianity than many a person in wealthy Europe. I visit the primitive operating room, where hundreds of deliveries and operations take place every year. The doctor's consulting-room is no larger than eighteen square feet. There are four wards full of beds for the poorest, and a tiny kitchen.

I see the spare-figured Indians who depended till recently on the favor and money of the landlords, who gave them advances on the proceeds of the cotton crop. The Church wished them to become independent and therefore taught them to help each other, to organize themselves and to free themselves from oppression and misery by cooperative projects. I visit the schools, the playing fields, the kindergarten, the agricultural institute, the cooperative bank. Everything has come into existence in a spirit of solidarity and cooperation. Everything is run by the generosity of volunteers without the money of the landlords or the intervention of corrupt politicians. Here the poor are their own masters. Here they assist themselves without having to bow their heads to unscrupulous grandees. And the Church is marching at the head of nonviolent revolution.

As the evening advances, Monsignor Expedito prepares himself for his weekly meeting, this time at the Fazenda São Luis, a farm about fifteen miles from the church. He loads his Jeep with helpers and rushes away into the dark. We follow him with difficulty. Occasionally Monsignor's rattling vehicle stops to pick up someone else. Two boys are standing on his bumpers. The roads are extremely bad. Motionless cacti stand like menacing sentinels. Above our heads sparkles the Milky Way. We drive through a dry river-bed. We visit a radio school where thirty-two adults and children are learning to read and write. The journey continues through the prairie. The road has ended. We are driving straight between the goal-posts of a football field. Then through a cattle-gate. At eight o'clock we reach the farm.

Around the Fazenda there is a confusion of donkeys, lean horses, trucks and people. Six hundred persons have come riding through the night, singing, confident in the Church that is calling them.

The organization is excellent. While the parish priest is speaking to the married people inside the farmhouse, the boys and girls sit on the ground outside in two circles around kerosene lamps. There is singing and laughter. There is a spate of questions and answers. There are young fellows with fiery eyes talking like "people's tribunes". The principles of trade-unionism and of cooperative organization are being explained. Instructions on hygiene and the growing of cotton are given. A part of the catechism is explained. In the meantime the little children are being kept quiet by a dark girl with a melodious voice. She is teaching them to pray. The farm is crowded with people. Not even a mouse can find room. Clusters of people are grouped before the doors and windows, listening attentively to Monsignor Expedito. Breathless silence alternates with roars of laughter.

After the group meetings, Monsignor shows slides on the whitewashed outer wall of the Fazenda. The projector is connected to the battery of his Jeep. Six hundred people are watching happily.

The meeting ends with a prayer. Small groups of people remain behind to discuss what has been said. Courting couples disappear behind the barn. The heavy engines of the trucks begin to rev up. Donkeys patter through the night. A song sounds in the distance, while our Jeep is sore put to follow the indefatigable Monsignor straight across the prairie, through the river-bed and across the vast, arid country still struggling with the problems of the nineteenth century.

Our forefathers in Europe did not solve these problems, so the Church lost the confidence of the poor. Here I have discovered a Church that knows its duty and is winning back that confidence. Isn't it an honor to be allowed to help?

A VISIT TO NISIA FLORESTA

They seem to be just three ordinary girls living in the humble house opposite the church. But on the table in the side room there are flowers before a tabernacle, and in the wardrobe there are nuns' clothes. The tumble-down rectory, in which no priest has lived for years, is now the home of the Sister Missionaries of Jesus Crucified, who took over this parish two years ago.

A great deal of water had flowed through Rio Grande before the Holy Spirit and Bishop Eugenio succeeded in finding nuns and gaining permission to try this experiment. Without the understanding of the Roman Curia, the nuns would probably still be in school and the parishioners outside the Church.

The parish of Nisia Floresta was until a short time ago one of the saddest out-of-the-way corners of northeast Brazil. With neither priest, doctor nor drugstore, with one qualified woman-teacher and 80 percent illiteracy, the community had entirely fallen into decay. There was no governor or political party who bothered about the eleven thousand inhabitants; these remained all the more docile as voters the more ignorant they were kept. Only the bishop, who spends all his energy on raising up the people, did not desert his city. Having no priests, he sent religious who were willing to follow Jesus in his abandonment.

Great sacrifices were asked of the nuns. They not only gave up their unpractical religious habits and the numerous customs sometimes maintained in convents with a holy obstinacy, as indispensable means to perfection, but they are obliged to do without holy Mass and were even deprived of daily Communion as long as the Holy See only very infrequently allowed them to distribute and partake of the Most High with their own hands. Only those who have seen the tears in Sister Iraci's smile when she told us that until her arrival in Nisia Floresta she had never lived a day without Communion can guess how difficult the nuns found it to share this poverty too with their parishioners.

They began by making acquaintance with each of their parishioners personally. By asking everyone for information, they not only got together the particulars for the parochial register but gained the assistance of numerous willing people for their work. They set up a parish council to help bear the responsibility for any initiative. They did not lose time by doing the teaching themselves but trained catechists to whom they entrusted the teaching of religion. They recruited a church choir from among the blackest sheep of the parish, who, to the astonishment of the elders and the awe of the young people, now set the tone in the sanctuary with the faces of First Communicants. The nuns arranged courses for boys, girls and engaged couples, set up societies for mothers and Mass-servers and organized teams to clean the church. Twice a week they go around with singers and guitars to give entertainment evenings in all the remote corners

of the parish. In addition they invite leaders of the trade union
and cooperative movement to take their turn in educating and
organizing the people. The nuns baptize the majority of the
children. They pray at deathbeds or take the sick by Jeep to a
hospital. They sing the Liturgy of the Dead in church or, if need
be, in a cottage if there is no money to hire the community
coffin for the corpse. Then every evening they ring the church-
bell and light the candles in their gleaming white church for the
lucernario, which consists of parts of compline, a Scripture reading, a talk by one of the nuns, hymns and God's blessing, which
Madre Marlene invokes over all her children. In this way they
are deputies for the priest, who visits the parish for Mass and
confession only on Saturdays, and that not every week.

All this I learned during a day of recollection in Natal, where,
with the help of an interpreter, I preached to twenty-five nuns
employed in the interior or in priestless parishes. I accepted with
pleasure the invitation to come and see for myself at Nisia Floresta
this new form of parish work, made financially possible by our
benefactors.

It is late in the afternoon when, sunburned and brown with dust,
we enter the town. In the middle of a scorching, sandy plain
stands the monumental church with its two blunt towers. We
kneel before the Most High, which had been absent here for
more than fifty years. The floor is as clean as a new pin, and the
walls, adorned with plaster ornaments, are spotlessly white with
here and there a touch of gold. Most of the ninety saints who
used to fill the house of God with a supernatural confusion have
left their high pedestals and have democratically descended
among the people. Scattered throughout the whole parish, they
now keep watch over houses, bridges, wells, schoolrooms, crossroads, meeting halls and other useful institutions needing their
protection. The notice-board above the holy-water font is covered with the drawings and colorful scraps that make it possible
for the parish news to be understood not only by the illiterate
but also by us. I see among others a photo of "Maranatha", the

Jeep given to the nuns by an American bishop, which, through the generosity of the parish of Wasserbourg (France), has received four new tires.

The nuns receive us with joy. They show us their tiny private chapel with the Blessed Sacrament; the parish secretariat with statistics and registers; and their primitive dwelling-place, containing a table, a couple of rickety chairs, a lopsided cupboard, rusty beds and ancient mattresses contributed by the people to furnish the rectory. Even the food, waiting on the table for us, was brought by the people: cornflour cakes, chicken, rice, beans, half a fish and manioc. The Mothers' League cooked for us. The neighbor, who has a refrigerator, supplied a jug of cold water. The nuns are used to living on Providence and are surprised at nothing.

Once, they were being visited by a parish priest. They did not know what to do as they had neither food nor money in the house. But toward noon a woman knocked at the door, bringing a roast chicken so that the nuns could sit down to table with their guest without further preparations. On another occasion they were without bread. Sister Any took the last money out of the table-drawer but decided first to do her meditation. When she was finished she discovered in front of the door, like a present from Providence, the loaf that an unknown person had put there. Only a week ago there was only coffee for breakfast and a letter from one of their fellow-nuns. Instead of breakfasting they read the letter together, and before they had finished it, a man brought food for the whole day.

All this is not surprising to someone who believes in Jesus Christ and his Gospel. It would be more surprising if God did *not* do such things and should abandon his children who work so hard for him. But many people have become too wise. They can calculate so well that they have reckoned to pieces both the Gospel and the childlike faith and trust in Providence. The miracles promised to those who believe and trust in God they no longer dare to expect. And they prefer another explanation of the Gospel rather than suppose there is something wrong with their faith.

These nuns live by faith, and in two years they have made a paradise out of the parish desert. They are deprived of much of what used to seem to them indispensable. Having always to be at everyone's beck and call, which makes a traditional convent life practically impossible, and the spiritual emptiness caused by the absence of the Eucharist, makes their lives very hard. On the other hand, they hear so clearly the demanding voices of the people calling them to a still more perfect life, and they receive such an unprecedented abundance of consolation and grace that they unhesitatingly consider this new form of life in the service of the Church a gain. They radiate happiness.

When the bell rang in the evening, the people came flocking to church. Inside the church I counted more than three hundred people. It is the same every day. Hymns were sung to the accompaniment of guitars. A young mother brought her baby to the altar. A dog stood motionless in the center aisle when Madre Marlene, dressed now in her blue habit and veil and fluttering scapular, took her position between the front pews and began to explain one of Saint Paul's texts. The multitude listened intently to her high voice reverberating through the silence.

When at the end of the *lucernario* I gave Communion to swarthy men, elderly mothers, young wives and many children, I was moved by their deep piety. God, who for fifty years had neither priest nor tabernacle here, wished to dwell abidingly in their hearts. Although they were only descendants of slaves, he does not despise them. That is why it is worthwhile for these sisters to leave their schools and mother-house to serve the Lord there where he is to be found, as he has said himself, among the poorest of his children.

Numbers of religious congregations founded in the nineteenth century for works of charity have partly lost their charitable character and are sometimes even superfluous. But in many countries the old nineteenth-century distress that calls for love is amply present. Here the authentic spirit of many congregations can be relived in a modern fashion. The nuns of Nisia Floresta have pointed the way.

ALAGADOS, PENGUINS AND A CARDINAL

The Alagados are the stinking marshes that separate Salvador, the handsome capital of Bahia, from the azure ocean. In the black, oily water, sheer misery had built dwellings for hundreds of thousand of refugees who were no longer able to endure the poverty and exploitation of the Brazilian interior. Their flight to the city bearing the name of the Redeemer of mankind ended in many thousands of ramshackle pile-dwellings standing between the sky and the mud, as there is no building-land anywhere else for them. They live in the company of rats and vultures. Their streets consist of rickety bridges and galleries of planks and poles connecting the huts. The sanitary arrangements consist of a hole in the moldy floor. Any child falling into the poisonous water is hopelessly lost. Those who are not used to the stench vomit within half an hour. The people's only hope is the garbage cart bringing waste food and scraps from Salvador to be thrown into the morass. In this way the city gradually creeps to the sea. The day will come when they will no longer be living in the mud but on the garbage. They are already dreaming of the little stone cottage they will then build.

The three penguins were natives of Patagonia but had been carried north by the cold gulfstream and washed ashore at Salvador and kindly housed in the zoo. A team of vets was busy day and night trying to save the displaced animals, for whom the change of climate would of course be fatal. A large firm offered the most modern air-conditioning system to keep them alive. The newspapers published a daily bulletin of their health. The whole city was full of sympathy. Though neither expense nor trouble was spared, the animals died. Since then the dead penguins from Patagonia are just as much forgotten as the hundreds of thousands of living people in the Alagados.

The cardinal was Dom Eugenio, whom we once helped as bishop without a cathedral in Natal and who then went to continue his work in Salvador and Rio de Janeiro, still without a cathedral. We are not aware whether he is interested in penguins, but we do know that humanization is for him the beginning of spiritual care. As long as there are people who seem not to be made in God's image and are no longer the lords of creation, as long as they remain deprived of freedom and independence, as long as they remain more helpless than animals, being the slaves of exploiters and the victims of natural forces, Cardinal Eugenio's pastoral care will begin with teaching men to become complete human beings, by breaking their fetters and by reforming the systems that do not serve but oppress mankind.

In his opinion the Church in primitive countries has a different task from the one it has in organized states. All educational, hygienic, economic and social duties neglected by governments, through inefficiency or because they are merely instruments of a merciless and egoistic ruling class, will be fulfilled in a Catholic country like Brazil only if the Church as teacher of the nations educates her children for this purpose. This means that the Church must take over the leadership, especially through its dedicated laymen, not of an all-destructive revolution but of the emancipation process of dehumanized humanity. This natural care, embracing the whole person, cannot take the place of super-natural care for a man's soul, but forms its indispensable foundation. Traditional parish work is worthless in this seething country without the no-less-traditional care that the Church must expend on the development of the whole human personality. Our friend Cardinal Eugenio has proved that he is able to realize his ideas with courage, prudence, tact and perseverance. We have promised to continue helping him.

TRANSISTOR RADIOS AND DEACONS

It is Sunday evening and already dark when we drive down the fairly-well-laid federal concrete road to the south. At the palm woods we reach the state road, which is considerably worse. After about twenty minutes we feel, by the still more violent jouncing of the Jeep, that we have reached the municipal road. *"Descendit ad inferos"* (he descended into hell), groans the parish priest when, after a highly dangerous bend, the fourth category of the Brazilian system of roadways starts torturing our backbones; we are jolting over a kind of unbeaten path for animals and courageous pedestrians, coinciding in part with a dry riverbed.

After an hour and a half we finally reach a remote bush chapel. It is one of the eighty-five outposts of this parish with one priest and a hundred and ten thousand souls every thousand square miles. We enter the T-shaped building. The roof—of rough rafters and a network of laths and sticks on which the tiles are laid—is an architectural hazard and makes a frightening impression. But the parishioners, almost three hundred, do not fear any danger from the work of their own hands.

They are proud of their chapel. Although a priest comes here only twice a year, they gather here every Sunday to pray. Some of them think it even worth a three-hour walk. There are more men than women. Many mothers carry babies in their arms. They surround the altar in a dense crowd. On the altar, between lighted candles, is just a small transistor radio. Beside the altar hangs a stable-lantern. Beneath this are a dozen boys and girls who can read. They follow the bishop's evening Mass, broadcast by Radio Natal, in the four lay missals that the parish owns, and they act as leaders for the singing and the responses. This is the Church of the poor, who hunger for God. It is a moving scene. Men, women, young fellows, girls and children kneeling and standing, praying and singing, listening and responding in complete unity with their richer brothers in the faith, who are filling the temporary church of the bishop-without-cathedral. There no longer seems to be any difference between the churchgoers in the city and those present in this humble bush chapel.

The bishop's sermon is addressed to the whole diocese. For every Sunday evening the priestless Christians gather together in hundreds of radio schools and bush chapels and join actively in the celebration of the holy Eucharist. The consecration is an impressive moment, when the motionless crowd hears the sacred words from the loudspeaker; and at the sound of the altar bell, they reverently make the Sign of the Cross.

While Communion is being distributed in Natal, the parish priest, who has today already offered up four holy Masses, whispers to us that he soon hopes to get permission to keep the Most High in his chapels. Then the faithful will be able to receive holy Communion from the hands of a layman during the radio Mass. This is a temporary solution. For after the transistor radios we gave him, which will henceforth be indispensable to him in his parish work, he is now impatiently awaiting his first deacons.

With the financial help of our ministry, those first deacons are being trained on the tiny island of Itaparica in All Saints' Bay near Salvador. Three days after our visit to the bush chapel, our journey leads us in that direction.

The azure-blue Bahia de Todos os Santos, which gave its name to the state of Bahia, lies smooth as a mirror in the burning sunshine. The one-time Portuguese fortress rising out of the water in the middle of the harbor seems to be uninhabited. Only two slender palm trees stand silently on guard. A white ship takes us to Itaparica, where the deacons' training course is being given in a ramshackle, empty seminary with red roofs, salmon-pink walls and picturesque pergolas surrounded by an earthly paradise full of coconut palms, breadfruit trees and century-old *mangueiras*.

Here we find the first nine candidates selected by their bishop to prepare for the diaconate. They are all of them mature men above age thirty, and mostly about forty years old, married and "successful" both in their marriages and in their careers. They have experience of apostleship and a certain economic stability and enough spare time for activities as deacon on Sundays and holy days or during the weekend. It is to be expected that they will all be accepted by priests and people. Their wives are able and prepared to accept and support their husbands' vocation.

It is a mixed company: two workmen, a police inspector, a town clerk, a tax-collector, a supervisor of an oil pipeline, a law clerk, a secondary school principal and a bookkeeper. The police inspector had his whole family vote on his decision; his wife and the majority of the family voted in favor of his becoming a deacon, on condition that he will devote at least one Sunday a month to his family. The wife of the pipeline supervisor, a coal-black man who is already very well known as a street-corner preacher, is so enthusiastic about the selection of her husband that she did not shed a tear when he set off on the long journey to Itaparica. The school principal, father of ten children, is at the same time a skilled musician and prepares the musical program for the diocesan radio station. He writes for two news-papers, plays the organ in churches where there is no organist and is the chairman of a committee preparing the formation of a philosophy faculty. The law clerk in his spare time manages all the real estate of the diocese and is the "John the Baptist" preparing the way in priestless parishes for nuns to come into action. And in this way each one of them has effectively proven his love for the Church.

The training course is given by the most capable professors and experts to be found in the whole of Brazil: five priests, two nuns and four laymen. Father Antonio, a Dutch Redemptorist, is astonished that his pupils can so easily assimilate the often very difficult subjects. Sister Maria da Cruz praises their attention and humility. All of them feel unprepared and long to be helped to interpret faithfully the teachings of the Church. They do not overestimate themselves and are deeply aware of the respon-sibility they are taking upon themselves. Their zeal is admir-able. This first month they are being given 108 lessons on the Scriptures, pastoral theology and ethics, Church history, liturgy, Church music, voice, sociology, psychology of teaching, com-munication media and the problems peculiar to the under-developed countries.

The entire course of training lasts twenty-five months, of which the first, the thirteenth, and the twenty-fifth months are

devoted to intensive study in Itaparica. They give up their holi-
days for this purpose, while our ministry covers the travel and
lodging expenses and also all expenses for the team of professors.
During the remaining twenty-two months the training is continued weekly by correspondence, and the candidates devote
themselves to practical diaconate work. Every month, together
with their wives, they make a day of recollection, when they
can exchange experiences. A priest and a layman, both experts,
are in charge of the trainees and visit them regularly, and also
their families, their parish priests and their parishes. After the
twenty-fifth month (the third intensive training month at Itaparica), those whom the bishop considers suitable will receive
their ordination as deacons.

They will have a threefold ministry. The ministry of the
liturgy: administering baptism, giving Communion, assisting at
marriages, giving the last sacraments, conducting funerals and
all religious services in the absence of a priest. The ministry of
preaching: teaching catechism, giving marriage and baptismal
instruction, ecclesiastical assistance to lay organizations and the
forming of public opinion. Service to the poor: this will not be
restricted to charitable activities but also includes basic instruction
and all forms of human advancement.

Originally, deacons were ordained to serve the poor. The
restoration of this office is a clear testimony to the Church's
desire to be the Church of the poor. It is probably the only
means of organizing Church life in districts where there are few
priests. It offers the only practicable possibility of satisfying the
inalienable right of the faithful to receive the bread of the Word
and of the Eucharist. It is an essential element of Church hierarchy. It has its own task and grants a special grace that the Church
in these times of total renovation cannot be without.

There is no doubt that the celibacy of the priests is of a precious
and indispensable value. But it is a charism not given to all of
God's children who are suited for an apostolic task. For them
the noncelibate diaconate opens the way to an apostolate. In
addition, the deacon's marriage adds more significance to the

celibacy of the priesthood. And both states in life bear witness to the freedom of the children of God.

The nine men of Itaparica will as deacons be neither priests nor laymen. They will have their own place in the hierarchy; they will be indissolubly bound to bishop and clergy. Their family life and their work will give them a place in the midst of the people. They will serve both.

On the tiny ship taking us back straight across the azure-blue Bay of All Saints, and past the sleeping Portuguese fortress to Salvador, we pray for God's blessing and the sympathy of our benefactors for this initiative. And we are waiting for new candidates, one of whom will be destined for the remote bush chapel where three hundred poor people are hungering for God.

THE CHURCH OF THE POOR

Much is being said about the Church of the poor, but I have discovered in the course of my wanderings through East and West that more and more poor people are feeling themselves abandoned by the Church. For countless victims of capitalism and Communism, the tragedy of the nineteenth century is being repeated—the oppressed are losing faith in the Church because she could not convince them that she was on their side. Consequently social leaders in Latin America are reproaching the Council fathers for having spared capitalism. Persecuted Christians in Eastern Europe are desperately disappointed that Communism has not been re-condemned. These are facts that must give us pause.

We who belong to the prosperous Church and are proud of being adult, know that the time for anathemas is past and that we are obliged, even without constraint, to translate the social teaching of the Church into action. But woe to us if we fail to do so. For we are a minority. The majority are the poor and undeveloped. If we neglect them, we make the Church an exclusive club in which there is no place for those in whose sorrow I have seen the tears of Christ.

This sorrow sometimes drives people to death. Such was the case with Severino Silva, the exploited Brazilian whose wife and children I visited at Macau the day after his death. He had been working for a salt company. For weeks the wages had not been paid. For the monies of the Compania Commercio e Navigaçao, who are exploiting the salt basins and the illiterate people of northeast Brazil, can more profitably be left in the bank in Rio than put in the workers' pay-envelopes. Thus it happened that on March 17, 1966, Severino had not a single cruzeiro left to buy bread for his children. Then, on the company's property, he soaked himself in gasoline and set himself on fire. He hoped that his death would be considered a labor casualty and that his wife would become entitled to a pension. Some time later I saw the luxurious head office of the Compania in the Avenida Rio Branco in Rio de Janeiro. On the pavement I prayed for Severino Silva and his family, and I beseeched the Lord of Hosts to destroy once and for all the monstrous survivals of nineteenth-century capitalism and to liberate the slaves of this Catholic country.

And I also thought of another slave. He was called Francisco Velazques and lies buried in Potosi in Bolivia. He had had four children and was nineteen years old when he died. Ten years before his death he had gone to the mine. The entrance lies at a height of fifteen thousand feet. Inside the mine the temperature is 90°F; and above the ground, 5°F below zero. Francisco Velazques died of black-lung disease, as do all the miners in that country.

When as a nine-year-old boy he went down the mineshaft for the first time, he was given a contract. He was paid by cubic meter. The mine advanced him the money for a pickax, dynamite and other working materials. In this way he became bound to the mine. He was small and frail and did not earn enough to pay off what the company had advanced him. But the company was patient, and he continued working. His loaded oar-truck weighed

225 pounds, and the rails were so worn out that it often derailed. This cost him time, and he earned less. But the company was patient and advanced him money for dynamite and oxygen cylinders.

At the end of six years he was attacked by the dreaded disease. If he had then quit the mine, he might have lived for another ten years. But his debt was not yet paid off, so he could not leave. His children were starving, and he went on working. His wife went to the city and sold coca and fruit. Sometimes he stayed down below for three days to work off his debt. This made the disease worse and reduced the amount he could produce. But the company gave him additional advances.

The longer he worked, the larger became his debt. He could not get away from the mine. His children died of hunger, all in the first year of their lives. He worked on, naked, with his feet in water. The mine was nationalized, but nothing changed except the debt, which kept on getting larger. When he died, he owed the mine company ten months' wages. He was buried in the community coffin, of which he could take only the bottom plank into the grave with him.

I was told this sad story in La Paz. There, opposite the cathedral, I saw the streetlight on which, during a revolution, the president had been hanged. It is a national monument guarded day and night by two soldiers. But the death of the president was of no avail to Francisco Velazques, just as little as was the revolution. Nor did the trade union, run by the Communists, help him at all. For its leaders are corrupt. Their power does not come from the workers but from the government or from the employers. They receive triple salaries and high bonuses. They live far away from the sweaty people, in luxury, and let the misery go on. The misery must continue, for it serves the world revolution. That is the dogma of the Communists.

The Communists hate the Church, which is here the only power to defend the poor. They menace the leaders who are working to raise the proletariat. They shoot at priests and social workers who are educating the illiterate people to become conscious activists with a knowledge of the social laws and the rights of the workers and who denounce the dictatorship of the trade union.

Francisco Velazques is buried at Potosi. God himself has dried his tears because he was the defenseless victim of an inhuman system. His mother stood at his grave and mourned. Don't say that his mother was guilty of his death. For his mother is holy Church, which is the only power in this country that honestly fights for the poor.

A BARON IN THE CALLAMPA

In Santiago, the capital of Chile, I made the acquaintance of Father José van der Rest. He is tall, fair, unshaven and fortyish. You cannot tell by his threadbare cassock and his unpolished shoes that he was born in a castle in Flanders and therefore received a French education. I was touched by the kind-hearted obstinacy with which for my sake he insisted on speaking the bad Flemish customary among Belgian barons. In his youth he attended a French-speaking Jesuit college in Brussels and was expelled from the school. Later on the Jesuits did admit him to the novitiate. This seems quite possible among the Jesuits. To his own astonishment his vocation held out. He is the Jesuit with the largest heart I have ever met, even though he is a university professor. Apart from this he is the parish priest of two parishes with eighty thousand souls, a manufacturer of houses and father to the neglected *callampa* youths.

The word *callampa* means "mushroom": in Santiago the slum areas are given this name because they shoot up overnight around the rubbish dumps like mushrooms.

When the priest was sent to Chile, he first lived for two years voluntarily in such a *callampa*, in just as primitive a way as the six hundred thousand others compelled to undergo this way of life in Santiago. He prayed and meditated in his hovel made of planks and clay with a rusty roof of flattened kerosene-cans. He himself, in swimming trunks, dug the deep hole that had to serve as a toilet. He helped the poorest to build their huts and made friends with the vagrant boys in the miserable mud streets and housed them in the "Hogar de Cristo" (House of Christ), of which he is the chaplain. Hundreds of abandoned and neglected children find a home here and are evaluated. The boys who are found to be adaptable are entrusted in groups of a dozen to a married couple and brought up as a family. In these families there is an atmosphere of happiness and peace such as I have seldom met with elsewhere. Father van der Rest has eighteen such families under his spiritual and material care.

For the boys of the large collective center and the eighteen small "houses of Christ", he set up a trade school where they can learn a trade and at the same time earn their living. They make soccer shoes, ironwork, hinges, musical instruments and coffins. These are simple coffins of thin planks, given away free to the poor, and also luxury coffins of expensive wood, with nickel fittings, bas-reliefs, zinc linings and plate-glass windows, which are sold at a high price to the rich. For years Father van der Rest has covered his expenses with this coffin shop. He had the largest coffin business in Santiago.

His special vocation is the manufacture of emergency dwellings according to a process invented by himself. On iron feet, firmly anchored in the ground, rests a steel framework in which the rafters and planks for the roof and for the walls are fitted. A space is left open for a door and a window. Everything is sawn to measure, and the young fellows assemble the ready-made walls and roofs without difficulty. They prefabricate dozens of cottages a day. These are afterward screwed together in the *ca-llampa*. The wood comes from the forests of southern Chile, and for the first few years was most probably stolen. Such a "prefab" house costs only twenty dollars. The money is collected by rather impudent begging.

Until a few years ago, Father José said three Masses every

Sunday in the street—he had no church—and after every Mass
he built a house, which he gave away to the poorest family in
the neighborhood. For he did not wish to preach about God
without giving some tangible evidence of his goodness.

I drove with this padre through the *callampas* of Santiago. His
Jeep had been badly damaged, not by an accident but by furious
Communists, who have repeatedly tried to destroy the vehicle,
which is in the service of the poor. But they have not yet succeeded. The Jeep still serves every day to carry the sick to the
hospital, to bring milk powder to the holiday homes, prominent
visitors to the *callampas* and corpses to the cemetery.

We visited first the poor living on the rubbish dump, who
were busy, around a small fire, salvaging old rubbish out of the
dumps. We climbed over granite blocks and broken masonry,
remains of houses and rubble left by earthquakes. It looked like
a fantastic moon landscape beside the dried-up river. In this dead
mountain scenery of rubble heaps, huts and caves have been built
of loosely-piled stones, complete with penthouse, fence, dog and
chimney.

We traverse an endless *callampa* between the railway embank-
ment and, lying around the hovels, a half-finished street with a
stinking moat full of viscous, gray mush crawling with fat beetles. The stench weighs on the lungs. Many children have rat-
bites. We creep inside a hut. The door is a little more than five
feet high and sixteen inches wide. Three adults and five children
sleep on moldy rag heaps covered with flies. On the roof is a
doll's cradle, and outside is a pot with poor-people's flowers
hanging on the wooden wall. The flowers are better off than the
people, who have to live inside. Oppressed and silent, we walk
around this concentration camp of wretchedness full of exploited
and outraged people.

In the city the national holiday was being celebrated, but in
this *callampa* we saw no flags or banners but only rags waving
on rusty lines in the wind, just tatters to cover nakedness.

Now and then the padre patted one of the miserable people
on the back in a kindly way—it was always the very poorest—

and said, "If you like, you can join us on Saturday night. At eleven o'clock, near the cathedral." After he had made this arrangement two or three times, I asked him: "But, father, what are you going to do at the cathedral on Saturday night?"

"Once a month we get together there, about thirty people whom I have selected. I look for a suitable piece of ground beforehand and bring the houses along with me. And then we build a new *callampa* in the night."

"Is that so? And where do you get the money to pay for the land?"

"I don't pay for it. We annex it."

"Annex it? Are you allowed to?"

"Of course I am", he replied. "I can't allow these people to be swallowed up in their misery!"

"And don't you get into trouble for it?"

"Oh, rather. I've been in jail three times already."

"And what do your superiors say to that?"

"Oh, they don't mind."

"What! Don't they mind?"

"Of course not, because the Cardinal backs us up."

"The Cardinal?"

"Yes, didn't you know?" And then he told me the strange story of "La Victoria".

A number of years ago a terrible fire broke out in one of the *callampas*; fifty thousand people lost their homes. A famous Jesuit, Father Hurtado, who has since died, wanted to profit from the occasion by building a model *callampa*. He looked for a piece of land with a water supply and drainage, because the fact that there is no water supply and no sewerage makes the hygienic conditions so bad that 70 percent of all the children die in their first year of life. He found a splendid piece of ground of some fifty acres with water supply and sewerage. Actually the government had planned to build a sports center on it, with a stadium, swimming pools and soccer fields. But the priest considered it more suitable for his model *callampa*.

He prepared the plan in deepest secrecy. Everyone had to bring his own building materials: planks, tin, straw and firewood. From an organizational point of view it was a first-class achievement. In one night he housed fifty thousand people on government property.

The next morning the whole of Santiago was in an uproar. The Jesuit was arrested, and the government sent troops to clear out the huts and bulldozers to plow under all the buildings—because this site was intended for a stadium. Then the Cardinal broadcast the following speech over the radio: "This priest is right, and so are those with him. For God has created the earth for the people who are the lords of creation. Those who have no living-space have the right to annex a piece of the earth for themselves. This is a law of nature and more important than a stadium. Therefore I demand that these people be allowed to stay in their dwellings and that the priest be released from prison."

It became a struggle for power between the Cardinal and the government, with the rights of the poor at stake. The Cardinal won. The hovels were allowed to remain where they were, and the priest was released. The victorious poor carried him in triumph around the *callampa*, which is still called "La Victoria".

I was very interested to meet this Cardinal. I talked for hours with him about his social and pastoral plans. On that occasion I learned that he had recently visited the strikers of Santiago. I had heard something about this strike and had seen the castle belonging to the factory owner. It was a luxury building with a golf course and swimming pool and two personal cows for the milk for his coffee. He was not in the least perturbed that his workers were living in misery. He considered himself to be infinitely superior to them. But the Cardinal went on foot to visit them during the lunch hour, when they were sitting on the pavement in front of the closed factory, eating their bananas and bread crusts. He had taken his own sandwiches along with him and ate them with the strikers in the street. He wanted to show them quite plainly on whose side the Church stood. I am grateful to God that I have met this Cardinal, to whom I have promised a quarter of a million dollars.

When he showed me out, there were twenty poor people waiting at his door. Not poor people such as you find in Europe, but stinking, filthy, half-naked wretches covered with sores and lice. I wondered what the Cardinal would do. He graciously took leave of me. Then he turned to the twenty poor people with the same graciousness and took them inside with him. With them Christ entered into his dwelling. I know that he will bless him and help him in the great battle he is fighting.

Father José van der Rest has become one of my best friends. Sometimes he turns up in Rome or in Tongerlo, lean, blond and smiling, with stains on his borrowed clergyman's suit and a grateful heart under it, in search of trucks, circular saws and benefactors, or to settle accounts and to thank us. Our friendship is of great importance both to him and to us. We discovered in him an apostle of action and an ideal partner to carry out effectively our relief plans for the menaced Church in Chile. As for him, he became so popular among our benefactors as a result of what we wrote about him that his life-work was given an unprecedented boost.

He still does a great deal of pastoral work with his hands. On sites that he annexes to the glory of God (recently he stole a cemetery), he conjures up endless rows of prefabricated houses, primitive wooden structures in which the poor can be temporarily housed. For the first time in their lives they are given a chance to live like human beings. Thus he organizes the gray, unmanageable masses of the subproletariat into workable groups who afterward unite, at his direction, into cooperative working- and building-communities who themselves undertake the further improvement of their living conditions. He scourges them awake in their own coarse language and chases them to work on Sundays after Mass with banter and abuse, to construct together with many of their fellows a better future.

The Jesuits of Santiago, under the leadership of Father Roger Vekemans, the son of a Belgian Communist, help him in every way they can. Their study center, partly financed by our ministry, is like a spiritual shipbuilding yard where the most daring socio-pastoral projects are launched, and is at the same time the brain of the cooperative movement that is educating the Chilean proletariat to independence. Father van der Rest is its charismatic animator. The economic and legal leadership is in the hands of a young lawyer with a famous name. His uncle is chairman in parliament. His father is a millionaire and owns nearly all the Chilean mines. He himself is twenty-seven years old, has given up his law practice and has persuaded his fiancée to put off their marriage for a few years. He is the solicitor of the poor, and fights with ministers and industrial tycoons for the acknowledgment of the rights of the poor.

Father van der Rest tells us all about these courageous friends in the broken Flemish that he still remembers from his youth in Belgium. His reports are impressive. Wooden cottages are being prefabricated in Santiago, Concepción, Valparaíso and four other places. His production of emergency dwellings has already far exceeded two hundred thousand. This means the beginning of a human existence for a million and a half of God's children. Dozens of priests live as poor men among the poor in the sand deserts in which Van der Rest is setting up his houses. They build their own cottages and accept no money for Masses and sacraments. They have been joined by many laymen who are living only for the kingdom of God. For years we have been supporting this apostolate.

Father van der Rest is above all a priest and does impossible things so as not to neglect pastoral work. Every Friday evening he drives from Santiago to Concepción with a truck-load of coffins. He arrives on Saturday morning after a journey of 325 miles and four hours' rest. He unloads the coffins in the warehouse. The truck, loaded with four tons of nails needed for the manufacture of his houses, is driven back to Santiago by another driver. He himself spends Saturday hearing confessions, baptizing, visiting the sick and restoring order in his home for the destitute in Concepción. On Sunday morning he celebrates Mass and preaches in the two chapels he has built for the *callampa* dwellers, and he solemnizes marriages. In the afternoon he takes the airplane back to Santiago, which costs him six dollars, and in the evening he is again a priest at the altar.

This wild Jesuit with the blue eyes of a child and an apostolic heart came to Europe a few years ago on a short visit. He had only very little time for his elderly mother in Brussels, for he had brought his concerns with him: his truck was wrecked, his power saws had lost their teeth and he was looking for a permanent source of income for his Hogar de Cristo. We not only gave him two trucks and new saws, but also a number of scooter-cars, which my friend Staf Vermeulen visited all the fairs in Flanders to collect. They are the first scooter-cars to operate in Chile. When they were introduced, it was a national event. Boys from the Hogar de Cristo exploit this new form of popular entertainment. The earnings are fantastic. Within a month the initial expenses were paid back. The income serves as a permanent financial basis for Father van der Rest's youth hostels, which gives him time and energy to extend his solution of the housing problem to other countries besides Chile.

CONVERSATION WITH CHRIST IN RIO

Black birds are swooping in wide circles around his head. His cloak hangs from his shoulders, and the hem of his pleated robe reaches his feet. That is how I saw Christ towering on the high mountain above Rio de Janeiro when I visited that city on my journey through Latin America.

Discouraged and depressed by the incredible misery infecting this Catholic continent like leprosy, I climbed the mountain to speak to you, Lord, in the name of the poor. On the way, my heart was filled with perplexity at the sight of the poverty of so many millions. Allow me to tell you, Lord, that what I have seen in this continent is a scandal. Conditions prevailing here are a disgrace to Christendom. Your Church is vulnerable here as nowhere else in the world. The battlefield where the future of your kingdom is to be decided lies in the hearts of the poor, who are left to their fate in this country. The decisive weapons are not atom bombs but faith, love and justice. Famine that was at one time, maybe, an accident is now an outrage. The poorest classes of the population have already discovered the abnormal and monstrous character of their misery in comparison with the luxury of the few living in abundance. The immediate juxta-position of blackest poverty and squandered wealth is the cause of the great awakening. I have heard revolution growling in the starvation areas of the northeast, in the coffee plantations of Colombia, in the tin mines of Bolivia and in all the universities of this fermenting continent. And I must admit, Lord, that this revolution is righteous because it is aimed against poverty, illit-eracy, social injustice and human despair. Here a process has begun that we may not restrain but must lead to its fulfillment.

And now I have arrived in this wonderful city where you are standing with outstretched arms on this mountain at the edge of the ocean. Is this the New Jerusalem that you are weeping over? Your expression is grave and melancholy. You see the ivory-white beauty of Copacabana nestling in the emerald cush-ions of the hills, against the softly breathing bosom of the sea. You see the luxurious city edged with golden beaches, blazing with yellow and ocher. The skyscrapers stand on slender legs in the middle of the sea of houses or close against the steep mountain flanks or in endless rows along the white surge of the ocean. A fine city, O Lord!

But you also look down upon the terrible *favelas*, the slums of the poor, struggling up on all parts of the slopes where the mountain is not suitable for modern architecture. Here the archi-tects of those in misery get their chance. They have taken rough possession of the slopes.

From this vantage point, where you command the heights so unassailably, the *favelas* resemble a strange mosaic in drab and black. But each spot of this menacing picture covers the misery of a whole family. Eight hundred thousand poor people live here. Fleeing from starvation, they left the interior to come to the golden city, but they have arrived in hell.

Yesterday I wandered through the *favelas* till late in the evening. A hundred yards high against the slopes the miserable hovels are piled one above the other. The lowest remain at a respectful distance from the spotlessly clean concrete street, but the filth of thousands rolls down unheeded. I pass through "streets" hardly more than two feet wide, where I have to squeeze between the hovels. Lord, you know how God's children are housed here, how violated and injured they are by their intolerable hardships. You saw how a drunken woman—she works in a bar and is paid in drink—spat in my face because I was not clothed in rags. You also know the grocer's tiny shop made of rotten planks, where the food is sold not by the pound but by the spoonful because these people are too poor to pay for more at a time. You can also see from here the tree between the stinking huts, straining and writhing toward the light and the pure sky. But what can the people do? They are suffocating in misery.

You know, Lord, that yesterday I walked away in despair out of the moldy hutch measuring nine by twelve feet in which twelve people live. The walls are papered with the cover-pages of illustrated papers, pin-up girls in bikinis, pictures of Saint Barbara and of Sophia Loren, of the famous Rio carnival and of the Holy Virgin. The tin roof of flattened tar-barrels is not water-tight. The air is thick with stench and music. Flies and naked children crawl on the ground. A sick girl lies on a worn-out mattress, covered with rags. Between this hovel and the next is a cardboard partition full of cracks and holes. Half-dressed young women peer from the window opposite. The huts are so close together that it is difficult to tell whether one is inside or outside!

Yes, Lord, I walked out, after a quarter of an hour, and was sick in the open air, like a dog. But I could do nothing for the family. Where they have been for sixteen years, they will have to stay. You know them, Lord! The father is named Miguel de Sousa Mendes, and his wife is Olivia-Maria. I even wrote down the names of the children for you: Gracia-Maria, Oswaldo, Francisco, Vera-Lucia, Zilda, Pedro-Paulo, Vicenti, Belmira, Esmeralda and Maria do Conceiçao (that is, Mary of the Immaculate Conception!). Aristocratic names of God's children, free-born, whom you have redeemed by your precious blood and who, in all innocence, are doomed to live in a hell on earth. They were born to misery.

Lord, it is inevitable that little Vicenti will in bitterness become a Communist when he gets to learn that his little sister Esmeralda has had to sell the royal splendor of her young body on the fashionable beach of Copacabana in order to survive.

Lord Jesus Christ, what are we to do? Why are the little girls in the far-off countries of Europe so much better off than Esmeralda is? Why need *they* not parade like long-legged gazelles before the millionaires who, quite close to the *favelas* in their clubs, swimming pools and casinos, squander the money they earned with the blood of the poor?

"Suffer little children to come unto me", was what you said long ago. But here on the mountain of Rio come only tourists and the sailors of an American warship lying at anchor in the port. It is true that they are children, too, and you are not offended by their toys, such as cameras and binoculars, or by the questions as to the height of your figure and the width of your outstretched arms. You can even put up with the fact that Johnnie Reefs from Milwaukee has scratched his name and that of his girl friend inside a large heart on the door of the chapel that forms your pedestal.

Of course, they are children gazing in amazement at your monumental dimensions, and then hastily they search their guidebooks for the next sight to be seen. They do not mean so badly, and I can quite understand that you are not offended. But Esmeralda and all the wretched children of South America have more right to you, because they are in greater need.

I know, Lord, that you are not to blame. We ourselves are to blame. On this mountain stands merely your image, a stone Christ dragged up the mountain piece by piece on the backs of donkeys. We ourselves have to be the living Christ. It is not your fault that we so seldom give you the chance to become the heart and driving-power of our lives. Take possession of us now, at long last, Lord, and give us the strength to radiate your goodness and love toward these poor brethren. Let it enter our minds that the worst danger is not Communism but the misery in which they live while we remain hard and selfish. Give us the generosity to renounce everything superfluous, not from fear of Communism, but from a Christian sense of duty. Compel us at last to show justice and love to all who curse your name because they do not recognize your goodness in us. And look down from your high mountain in Rio onto our tiny Europe and bless it, that it may become great in love.

São Gonçalo, Brazil.

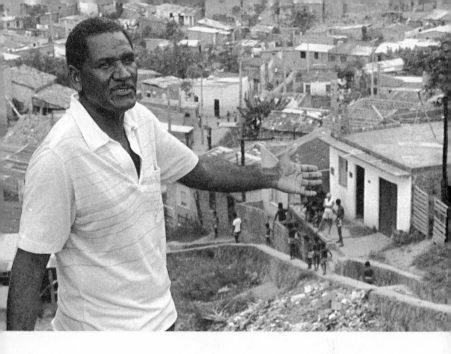

▲ Fr. Mauricio Abel pointing to his church in São Gonçalo, Brazil.

▼ Father and sons, São Gonçalo, Brazil.

An open-air Mass (there is no church) in Cryola, Peru.

This little girl lives in Peru.

Memorial of a campesino shot by the military in Peru.

In Africa

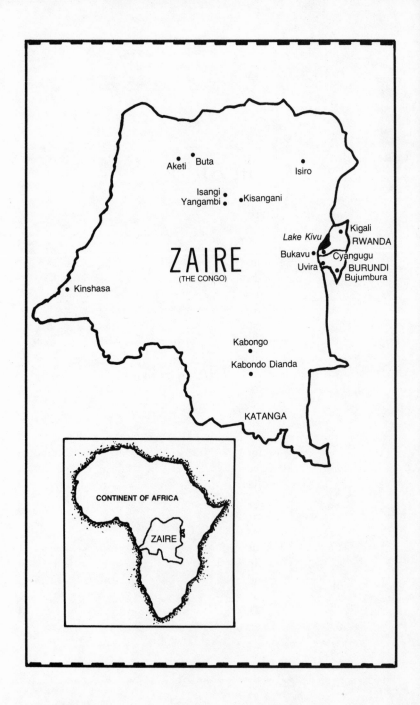

April 1965. We are flying at a height of seven and a half miles. The black cloak of night is resplendent with strange constellations. In the depths a fire glides past us. It might be hunters on safari, perhaps a village in the Cameroons. Lightning from a tropical thunderstorm strikes near the equator. Sheet lightning in a trembling blaze across the horizon makes the sky pale. It is night over Africa. Straight through this night I am flying from Rome to Kinshasa. The journey lasts six hours.

On the Kinshasa airstrip Father Jan Engelen stands waiting for me. He is the Tongerlo Abbey's mission procurator and leader of our newly formed African department. As regular superior and vicar-general of the diocese of Buta, he has been for years the consultant of colleagues and Congolese. He has thirty years' knowledge and experience of the Congo. He also knows the irresponsible game played with it by swindlers and dilettanti. He has suffered under inexpert decisions. That is why he has become taciturn in Europe.

But here he is in his element. In spite of the total disorganization, which is a consequence of Congolese independence, he has succeeded—thanks to diplomacy, Flemish obstinacy and the help of some American friends—in drawing up a breathtaking travel program. For nine days he will dish up before me the menu of misery. Hitchhiking in C-130s, we shall roar for more than seven thousand miles in the scantily lighted interiors of American super-transport planes, seated among gasoline barrels, powdered milk and Land Rovers, across the sky above the blood-red equator. Kinshasa, the starvation country Kivu, Isiro and deserted Kisangani are the stations of the cross where we shall meditate in perplexity how it was possible that an innocent people could be so sold, betrayed, exploited, downtrodden and destroyed.

Everybody agrees that conditions in the Congo are incomparably worse now than they were before. The number of white people has increased but their moral standards have fallen alarmingly. One who is in the know declared that the percentage of "white trash" is four times as high as it was under the Belgian regime. A Congolese church dignitary assured me that his people were swindled by an independence from which other people pick the fruits.

Now that the socio-economic defense ring that the Belgian administration had built around this underdeveloped nation has been demolished in the name of independence, and with the moral support of Communism, it is at the mercy of an unbridled and merciless capitalism. Unhampered, the strongest, the most cunning and the most conscienceless people can now exploit the defenseless masses. The people are relapsing into economic slavery. Capital is leaving the country by millions. Swarms of plunderers and profiteers have swooped down on the country like vultures.

At the last moment they are endeavoring to scrape together and bring into safety a loot of millions. Most of the black leaders are doing the same. Almost every function is hastily being exploited in order to fill their own pockets and to benefit friends and fellow-tribesmen as much as possible. Very seldom does care for the public welfare extend farther than the limits of the tribe to which the politician belongs.

There is no authority to defend the people against bloodsuckers and against themselves. Gold, diamonds and ivory disappear out of the country in whole plane-loads. A native monsignor cautioned me not to send money to certain Congolese authorities, as I could just as well send it directly to a numbered Congolese account in Switzerland.

High authorities invest their stolen millions in the Riviera nightclubs and send their secretaries and dozens of discarded concubines there. Traffic in women is a flourishing business. For a few pounds of rice, secondary-school girls sleep with Katangese soldiers and South-African mercenaries to keep themselves and their families alive. Twelve-year-old children are acquainted with all the symptoms of venereal disease. The exemplary Belgian socio-medical system, which was called an exorbitant luxury by indifferent UN officials, has been suspended. Doctors work without medicines and without salaries. Chaos reigns in the hospitals. The social scandal of polygamy has been publicly reinstated by ministers and directors of social affairs.

This is becoming a litany of want, sorrow and treachery. It is the sad story of the poor people of the Congo and an appeal to everyone willing to help raise it up out of its misery.

WE HAVE SEEN HELL

We are sitting on the veranda at the house of my friend Christian Sarre, who is a teacher of religion in Kinshasa. While Father Engelen is explaining our nine-day itinerary and preparing me, with an emphatic waggling of his beard, for the surprises and ambushes that are now the order of the day in the Congo, two Congolese are approaching along the wide avenue, looking for something. They are examining the numbers on the houses with great attention. Tired and exhausted, they seem to drag themselves along. You can read starvation on their faces. They are two fugitives from the rebel areas: two of the ten thousand who are suffering, waiting and dying in the slum quarters of Kinshasa.

When they discover Father Engelen, they begin to dance with joy. Without much hesitation he recognizes in them Ignace and

Roger, former parishioners from Aketi, the flourishing mission station where he had been the superior for eleven years. They had happened to read in the newspapers that he was staying in Kinshasa. They had been looking for him for a week, scattered sheep looking for their shepherd. Their meeting after an absence of five years was very touching.

Sitting quite close to the priest, with their knees against his, they tell him about what has happened to them. They belong to a prominent family of the Bofulas. Their grandfather, an old chieftain on whose head the Simbas had set a high price, was betrayed by people of his own tribe. A boy of thirteen was forced to finish him off with a revolver after indescribable tortures. Then it was their father's turn. Members of the family had delivered him over to the rebels. Children who had been hypnotized and intoxicated with hemp-fumes killed him with lances and cut him to pieces. The same thing happened to their uncle.

They also report the martyrdom of Jan Engelen's friend Leopold Monzikatebe, who was condemned to death by a people's tribune at Buta. Before the execution the Simbas wanted him to kneel down in honor of Patrice Lumumba, the god of the blacks. Leopold refused, saying that he wanted to die only for Jesus Christ. In the agony of his martyrdom he forgave his executioners. Struck by seven bullets, he fell to the ground in the midst of his prayer. Only when the Simbas cut the heart out of his body did he die. While his heart was being divided and eaten, his body was drenched with gasoline and burned. They took away his ashes to be used as a charm.

Hunted like wild animals, Ignace and Roger with thousands of others then sought refuge in the forest and stayed there for four months. They try to remember the names of the women and children who died of hunger and disease. They mention the names of friends and relatives who were slaughtered like cattle. They do not know where their mother and pregnant sister, who got lost in the forest, might be. They still shudder when telling about the massacres.

The law of the rebels was the law of the leveler. Everyone who was well educated or had a higher social position than the masses was cut down. Those who wore shoes or a clean shirt were beaten to death. Not a single natural structure was respected. Schoolchildren were compelled to murder their teachers, and children their parents. Everyone was terrified of his neighbor. The unity of the tribe, the foundation of African society, was deliberately destroyed. It was the collapse of a whole world. With panic in his tortured eyes, Ignace—six months after the terror—chokes out the words: "We thought the end of the world had come."

These terrible events cannot be undone. The spectacle of the martyred, who, before they were killed, were forced to swallow their own cut-off ears and genitals, will haunt the dreams of the survivors like a nightmare. They were forced to attend the execution of those who were dearest to them with dancing and hand-clapping. They will remember to their death the pungent stench of the tortured, who were made to drink themselves full of gasoline before they were cut open alive and set alight. They will carry this mental burden for the rest of their lives.

Only those possessed by the devil could have succeeded so radically in turning nature against itself so that coming generations, as if burdened by a new original sin, will be fated to live on in a spirit of pitiless vengeance and carry on the feud. The ones who will profit by it are the neo-imperialists who without any difficulty will rule these divided people who have relapsed into barbarity. In this lies the root of the hypocritically propagated decolonization. Here the swindle of independence comes to light. Here we discover, step by step, the traces of Chinese Communism and of Arab expansion policy.

It is no coincidence that the rebels are in possession of Chinese arms and instructors. It is not by any chance that Arab countries support the rebellion; that the standard-bearer of the revolt is an Arab-Congolese half-caste tribe, the Bakusu; and that the campaign of the Simbas followed the traditional road of the Arab slave-hunters. Peking and the Arabs are working hand in hand to conquer this continent and to exploit it at the expense of a defenseless people. Great is the responsibility of the leaders of the free world for not having had better insight or for having closed their eyes to what was happening.

The only power that has taken a realistic standpoint in these problems is probably the Church. The Church is no novice in the field of development aid. With the rich experience of ten thousand missionaries, she has placed herself, without naïve illusions, but altruistically and humbly, at the service of the young nations. In the Congo, too. She still hopes to be given the chance to train new officers and leaders who, inspired by true Christianity, will be able to create on the foundation of the African idea of society, modern and at the same time typically African ways of life. In this lies a task for our program, which has also adopted the menaced Church in the Congo in its relief efforts. We not only want to help the dioceses ravaged by the Simbas in their spiritual and material work of reconstruction, but to invest especially love, money and ideas in the training of apostolic-minded lay leaders.

In our attempt to fulfill this task, the past cannot be denied with impunity. The work of our missionaries, which may have been relatively on too grand a scale for Africa, but who themselves have with love served this country in their thousands, may have been left in ruins; but in the heart of this childlike people, love for the white missionary will remain indelible. This fact is of fundamental importance for the future. It opens the road to a renewed contribution of the European missionaries toward the reconstruction of the Congolese Church, which, humanly speaking, is doomed to destruction without them.

One often hears bitter criticism of earlier missionary methods. Such criticism comes rather late in the day and applies current standards to the entirely different situation of former times. It is criticism that springs from the Christian inferiority complex, which has become a fashion with some people. It is not based on truth. I did not find this criticism in the grateful eyes of Ignace and Roger, nor any complaint against the white priest who taught them, baptized, exhorted, chastened and loved them. They honor him like their father. They cling to him with boundless trust. He is the only one with whom they feel safe and protected. Naïvely they asked him if they could always stay with him.

The spontaneous reaction of these two poor fugitives and of dozens of others, when they again saw the old veteran Jan Engelen, proves that the ordinary population has other ideas than do those who rashly pass judgment on the guilt and responsibility of the previous missionary generation. For there are thousands of Jan Engelens who have served the Church in the Congo, not with unproven, ephemeral theories but with the self-sacrificing actions of a whole lifetime. Try to imitate them!

We may not write off the Congo as a bad debt. If primitive tribes were not able in seventy years to follow the routes it has taken us twice-seven-hundred-years to learn, in spite of their automobiles and European clothes, and suddenly relapse into barbarism, this was not the result of natural tendencies but of the fact that they were misled by wicked men.

This is why we ought not to dwell on the atrocities of a revolt, partly a consequence of the social chaos of an ungovernable republic and partly launched by Communist and Arab agents. Trusting to Providence, we should set our hands to the plow. And in recognizing our weakness, we should pray often and fervently. For the words that Roger spoke to me as we took leave sounded like a message from God in my ears: "We have seen hell and we ask you to tell them in Europe that the Church must pray for the souls of those who were innocently murdered and for the living to understand that Communism brings misery and death."

HUNGER IN KIVU

Unfolding itself beneath the worn-out DC-4 taking us in five hours from Kinshasa to Bujumbura is the green and endless map of the Congo. From the shiny-black minister who delayed the flight of the Air Congo airliner for two hours on account of a meeting, to the Italian refugee bishop of Uvira waiting for us some thousand miles farther east, our flight takes us straight across the Congo.

The old airplane wobbles like a rowboat on the high seas and rattles as if all the bolts are loose. Across the monotonous land-scape of clouds, forests, savannahs and jungle its swift shadow follows us like a strange reptile. The pilot has drawn his course with a ruler across an atlas. At intervals of some seventy to a hundred and forty miles we pass over a couple of fields, carefully cut out of the forest, with a collection of small huts looking like mudpies against the ground. A shaky child's hand has drawn a red path from the village; the path loses itself hesitatingly in the forest. Who is interested in this green hell? However, deep under the surface lie treasures that arouse covetousness.

Bujumbura is the capital of the republic of Burundi. After the customs formalities we continue our journey in a smaller airplane to the republic of Rwanda, where there is at Shangungu the only airport with a free approach to Kivu. All the other roads to this province are cut off by the rebels.

During the midday meal with the fugitive bishop of Uvira, whose eyes still reflect the horrors he has been through, we talk about Pistoia, his native town, where I have recently been preach-ing and collecting money, and of the distress of his ravaged diocese.

When the Simbas passed through Kivu, burning and murder-ing as they went, fifty thousand Congolese saved themselves by flight to Burundi. They escaped the fate of the Uvira Christians who were not able to escape and whose frightfully mutilated bodies were irradicably branded in the bishop's memory. I have seen the photographs and was astonished that relatively few of the witnesses who survived this barbarous event became insane.

Now that the Simbas have encamped in the mountains, the refugees are slowly returning to their wasted fields and their torn-down huts. They have had to eat up their seeds and roots so as not to starve. There will be no harvest this year. The bishop shows me newspaper reports on the distress in which these people live. Death is creeping through the banana plantations; the children have no milk; there is no salt; there is no palm oil. This situation gives rise to terrible and disgusting scenes. The press agency in Kinshasa (the D.I.A.) reports that the starving are opening the graves of the victims and are feeding on the remains of the corpses. There is danger of epidemics. There are no medical supplies and no doctors. My story is getting monotonous, although want takes on many shapes.

Here is another story. It was told me by a missionary nun. Full of pity for the fate of the starving children, she, with twenty-one other nuns, had evolved a plan to hire themselves out on two free days as pickers in a tea plantation. With the money they earned they would buy fish and distribute it among the hungry people. For fish is the only protein-containing food to be obtained in Kivu. Without fish and without the powdered milk sent by the Americans, no child can survive the famine.

The twenty-two sisters, black and white, picked tea for two days. They picked from early morning till late afternoon. The whole group picked forty-four complete working days. They picked with diligence and love, knowing why they were doing it. By tea-picking they hoped to conquer death. But when the wages were paid, each nun earned no more than forty francs for two full working days. For the work of the whole group they received nine hundred francs. Not Belgian francs, but devaluated Congolese francs, worth fifteen Belgian centimes. This meant that their collective wages for forty-four days of tea-picking had the purchasing power of only three dollars. And fish in Kivu is expensive. So death was not cheated of its harvest.

The fact that the plantation owner gave the sisters a couple of thousand francs extra for their charitable purpose makes no difference at all. The point here is that starvation wages are being paid from which not a soul can live. Moreover, I was assured that the tea was sold abroad at a quarter million Congolese francs per ton. The high official who connives at this receives a bribe of twenty thousand francs for every ton of tea that leaves the Republic tax-free. It is the same thing with quinine.

This is robbery on a large scale, out of all proportion. The tea is exported at two hundred fifty francs per kilo, less the twenty-francs bribe for the customs. The remaining two hundred thirty francs go into a planter's pocket. The picker earns seventy-five Congolese centimes per kilo and picks, at the most, forty kilos a day. This means for her a maximum wage of 0.3 percent of the selling price! It is not difficult to understand that the planter can afford a little charitable extravagance to ease his conscience now and again!

There is no doubt that every enterprise in the Congo has now become a matter of risk. Bankruptcy waits outside the door. The whites who have worked here for years—and not only for their own profit—have suffered and lost a great deal. Quite a number of them have become embittered. We can understand that, as down-to-earth businessmen, they want to save their capital before everything goes bankrupt. But this does not justify them in doing wrong. What is being done here is a crime that cries to heaven, for which there is no possible justification. The helpless inhabitants, born in the country and obliged to earn millions for foreigners by the sweat of their brows, are being deprived by a horrible conspiracy between white blood-suckers and corrupt Congolese authorities of the possibility of feeding their children and keeping them alive. This is preying upon living people. A nation is being massacred here.

These people are deserving of better things. for it is owing to their heroic courage that Kivu, although surrounded by rebels, is still free. When the inglorious national army, full of fear and superstition, fled before the oncoming Simbas, the tribal chiefs called the men to arms. They entered the mountains with lances and bows and arrows. They defeated the rebels in bloody battles and liberated the country. The triumph was dearly bought. The heaviest toll that had to be paid was the destruction of the harvest and the impossibility of preparing the field for the next year. That is why there is now starvation in Kivu.

To crown it all, the national army returned. The soldiers are well paid but lack all discipline. Like well-nourished parasites, they are sucking the last life-blood from the country. Together with the profiteers of the Congolese administration they are eating up all the food, which, to the very last kilo, has to be brought by plane via Shangungu. Under the guise of requisitioning or by impudent theft they are robbing the emaciated population, which with its last reserves is losing its will to live, its courage and its resistance.

Because of this system, which has been applied ever since the day of independence more or less throughout the whole of the Congo, a climate of disappointment began to prevail, which has greatly promoted the revolt of the Simbas and bears the seeds of fresh troubles. It is therefore not surprising that the young Mwami Mwesa III, whom I visited in Walungu, has only a dim view of the future. He does not think that it will be possible to call up his people to fight against the Simbas for a second time. The latter are being trained behind the mountains in the use of new weapons. The weapons come from China.

The government closes its eyes to all this. For whoever is in power profits by it as long as he can. He may not think of tomorrow. Thus it could happen that when a prime minister was received at Bukavu, an official dinner for five hundred guests was given. It cost seven hundred thousand francs. But at the same time oil was being sold on the market of Bukavu by the spoonful and rice by the glass because the supplies were exhausted. For a kilo of rice, two days' wages had to be paid. These poor people fell victim to independence. Bereft of all friends, they have been betrayed not only by strangers but also by their own leaders. Passive and helpless, they have been handed over to a conflict of interests, which takes into account everyone's interest except theirs. As their last resource they have the Church, which has been called to be the mother of the poor. In this afflicted land of hunger she must raise her voice. If she remains silent, she will lose the confidence of the downtrodden and will have betrayed her vocation.

THE BLOND DEATH STORY

And then came Mother Hadewych of the Holy Sepulchre, this little iron nun with the golden heart who, in the middle of the chaos of the interior, at Walungu, rules with a firm hand her convent, hospital, schools, tribal chiefs, orphans and a flock of native sisters.

Father Jan Engelen has known her for years. After a number of clashes they have managed together to extend the famous mission of Aketi so that it has become a pearl in the crown of Tongerlo and of the Canonesses of the Holy Sepulchre. For eleven long years they have worked and fought together shoulder to shoulder as superiors. Two sturdy characters as true as a die, uncomplicated and unbending. True-blue missionaries, who of all the pious trappings of their years of spiritual training have kept only what is essential and useful, but who have acquired through the storms of a hard life the true spirit of the evangelical counsels. That is why they have remained true religious to the very marrow of their bones, although their masculine language and frank judgment on matters of minor importance sometimes disturb the calm surface of the convent atmosphere.

Mother Hadewych accompanies us along incredibly bad roads to the remote mission station where her fellow-nuns are awaiting us, full of excitement. Barbed-wire barricades are dragged aside and barriers are raised to let us pass. Savage-looking soldiers salute the tiny nun respectfully as, undaunted, she leaves the army-occupied area with two white priests and Philippe, the driver. We drive past burned-out car-wrecks and gutted bungalows; a patrolman watches us go. We drive through a far-flung, virgin landscape.

In the folds of velvety green mountains, on plains and in valleys, we see the serrated leaves of banana plantations waving in the cool breeze that comes from the direction of Lake Kivu. Although the rust-brown roads are crowded with people, mostly women carrying their heavy loads like beasts of burden, we see no huts. These are concealed in the banana woods; ashamed of the misery they cover, their occupants do not wish to compromise the glory of this paradise with their poverty.

There is not a single cabin here where the angel of death is not silently crouched near the smoldering fire. He has his own place in the circle of the living. His name is *Mbwaki*—that is, "Undernourishment"—and his garments have the color of flax. For each tiny wooly head that he caresses becomes fair, and every jet-black little face that he kisses grows white.

The angel Mbwaki performs his task among all little children who can quiet their hunger only with sweet potatoes and a piece of banana. As soon as he sees that their dark pigment is disappearing through lack of proteins and vitamins, he takes them sadly into his arms. He waits until the tiny bellies are inflated and until the little feet swell up into unrecognizable lumps of flesh. He grieves when the curl goes out of their hair and when the all-devouring dermatitis attacks their little bodies like leprosy. Then he counts the wounds and falling hairs until the white froth sprayed on their gasping mouths reveals that the days of their torture are fulfilled. When all is over, he closes the bloodless eyes and turns weeping to the other children waiting for him to pick them like little flowers for death.

Please don't think I am exaggerating. What I have written is only a feeble description of the reality. Nor did I wish to believe these things when I was told about them. But when Mother Hadewych took me over hills and vales to the banana woods in which the huts lie hidden—when we ourselves had crept around the stinking huts looking for food but not finding anything but skinny children with legs like dry sticks—when we saw a child die of hunger before our very eyes, while the father was already behind the house, plaiting the mat for the child to be buried in—when five minutes later we saw a man with a dead child in his arms and a woman with a spade on her shoulder, passing like frightened animals along the forest path to return the fruit of their love to the earth—when I saw the parade of the six hundred pitiful little wrecks already marked by Mbwaki, who every day drag themselves to Mother Hadewych to receive a pint of milk—when I had read the names of the four thousand lovely, curly-headed little children who have died of starvation in this district these last two years—it struck me that God will curse us if we do not, all of us, do our utmost to remove this scandal from the most luxurious garden of Africa.

I know very well that Aid to the Church in Need is not a charitable organization. Our task is one of caring for souls. But I know also that Christ condemned a minister of religion because he neglected his duty toward his neighbor on the road from Jerusalem to Jericho. And again, Christ himself multiplied bread to feed the hungry, because he would not speak of God to people with empty stomachs!

The story of the Blond Death in Kivu is not yet finished. But before we tell it further we must bow our heads in pity for the dead children who were thus cruelly left to die, and for the remaining poor creatures who, being creatures of God, have a right to have their lives respected.

They have strange names: Cirhulwire, Mushagalusa, Naka-tiya. These mean Sweet One, Source of Joy, Tenderness. Are they to be added to the list of the four thousand who starved to death and whose souls cry to heaven for vengeance? Or can we appease God's eternal wrath by desperately trying to save their lives? Woe to humanity if we are too late. Woe to us if we fail in generosity. Woe to you if you do not understand that the life of the poorest black-skinned child is worth more than the prosperity you so undeservedly enjoy.

Katalana, Cibubulanda and all the other children whose names I read in the Walungu death-list are as dear to God as the children of Europe or America. And the black mothers whom he blesses with fertility taste the same joy as white mothers when their days are fulfilled and they press their child to their hearts for the first time. For the color of the skin does not change the heart of a mother. And the mother in Kivu who enters the forest with a spade to bury Cirhulwire feels as much sorrow as the mother in Boston who follows her child to the cemetery by car. For the color of her skin does not alter a mother's sorrow. And the mother who sees in helpless terror that her black-haired Mushagalusa is growing blond because of Mbwaki has as much right to her child as the mother in London who has sufficient milk and money to see her little boy grow into a strong man. For the color of her skin does not affect a mother's rights. Think now of the baby that is yours or that you would like to have, or that you carry through life as a fair memory. The baby with pink fingers and sparkling eyes. The child in your womb, at your breast or in your arms. The baby in the cradle. For the sake of this child and of all innocent children in the world, I would ask for justice and love for the children in the country of the Blond Death. What is your answer? From this answer will depend whether little Makatiya can go on living as a lively, playful child under the blue skies of Kivu—or whether her sorrowful father will soon have to be plaiting that mat for her funeral.

THE MUD-DWELLERS OF BUKAVU

The Congolese parish priest of Bukavu shakes his head despairingly when he re-enters the room. A little while before he had been called outside by three parishioners who did not dare go home because they had no food for their children. But the parish priest is just as powerless to cure hunger as the vicar-general, who has had a high fence set up in front of his house because the stream of starving people made it impossible for him to do any work. Now at least they cannot knock on his door. He cannot help them anyway.

The parish priest is young. He studied in Rome and is a doctor of theology. Before he becomes a seminary professor he wishes to learn from his own experience what are the needs of his people.

He is one of the best black *abbés* I have ever met. He is devoted body and soul to his enormous parish. He has a hundred thousand souls under his care, among whom are countless numbers of refugees and swarms of children. Many families have ten, twelve, even seventeen children. He baptizes forty a week.

The school is one of his major problems. A great many classes are taught in the open air. The number of pupils varies from 90 to 113 per class. The teaching varies with the number of pupils. The more there are accepted, the less they learn. But the fewer children admitted, the more the embitterment of the parents and the larger the number of illiterates, who are a threat to the future of the country. No schools have been built here since independence. As a matter of fact, there is no building done at all. For this reason and because after the departure of the whites the house-boys were left idle, 90 percent of the population is unemployed. There is no unemployment benefit for those without work. Some of them farm a small piece of land, but the refugees have no land and therefore no chance to keep themselves alive in a legitimate way. There are families that get a meal only once in two days and even then without satisfying their hunger. In this way it is not only the children but also a steadily increasing number of adults who are becoming victims of Mbwaki and becoming blond through undernourishment. The next generation is being threatened in its very substance. In the Bukavu hospital, twelve children died of undernourishment the day before.

Together with this black parish priest and the Belgian matron of the social center, which is entrusted to a fine AFI (Auxiliaires Féminines Internationales) group, we visit the refugees in the Nyamugo quarter. With difficulty we climb a lead-colored slope to which numbers of hovels cling in an inexplicable manner. These are shapeless contraptions made of small pieces of wood and red clay, sticking like bloodstains to the rocks. Fastened to a tree and a couple of protruding rocks is an inhospitable shed a little larger than the others. Above the door is painted the sign "Hotel". Wherever the slope offers a narrow ledge, we see an eruption of straw pustules rising from the broken clay-surface of the mountain. These are called cabins. They are too crude for pigs but are swarming with people. Black, friendly, patient people who hide their misery and despair behind a smile. Children of the sun who do not make a demonstration of their hunger. Only when the parish priest politely asks a gray-headed, rag-covered man if he will receive me in his hut does the latter whisper in the priest's ear that he has no food. This is not a complaint but an excuse for not being able to obey the law of hospitality. Rarely have I met people who are able to bear their poverty with such dignity.

I receive permission to visit the hut. I creep inside on hands and knees. Besides the ash-gray grandfather, his son and daughter-in-law and their six children live here. To the left of the entrance there is a smoldering fire. The emaciated little ones seem to be asleep, but their wide-open, ghost-like, shining eyes prove that they are awake. They are no longer "débutants", which is the hospital word for children who are at the initial stage of under-nourishment. These little victims of starvation are farther advanced on their way to death. They remind me of the quiet, helpless little bird I found in the snow when I was a boy. It died in my hand and had the same terror in its eyes.

On the rough, clay floor lies the iron lattice-work of an old cement sieve. This serves as the bed for the very smallest child. The others sleep on straw or in a kind of hammock. Behind the tatters of a half-decayed piece of canvas I notice a nest of dried grass. Here the parents sleep. On the dirty cloth I can read the half-effaced letters of the French word "Restauration". There is certainly a great need for restoration here. Did Saint Paul have this misery in mind when he wrote of God's plan to restore everything in Christ? He certainly was not thinking of the restoration of Christian cultural monuments. Millions are being spent on these. But God is not served by the restoration of paintings and cathedrals as long as his very countenance continues to be reshaped beyond recognition in the pitiful grimaces of starving children. When shall we finally learn the lesson taught us by the symbolic act of Pope Paul VI in selling his tiara: that all the balderdash of ecclesiastical treasures, cloth-of-gold vestments and imposing manifestations, all the treasures of Christian art, all triumphs of Christian civilization, nay even science, faith, the gift of prophecy and martyrdom at the stake are without any value as long as we refuse God the love he is waiting for in the persons of the least of his children—among whom are these children in the stinking hut of Bukavu?

I can bear to stay only a few minutes in this nine-foot den. There is no chimney. White-ash particles float through the place and irritate my nose and throat. The smoke burns tears out of my eyes. Or am I crying because of the six children? When I am once more outside and turn around, I see smoke escaping out of the straw roof. The hut looks like a smoking dung-heap. In this dung-heap live nine people created by God to become lords of creation and to rule the earth.

And yet this family lives in luxury compared to the outcasts whose ground lies athwart the slope and therefore does not allow of building straw huts. Those outcasts contrive shelters that have to be seen to be imagined. There is no possible kind of material that cannot be stolen and used for these architectural monstrosities. The rusty tin roofs, cut out of kerosene cans and held in place by stones, are as red as the mud with which the holes in the wall are filled up. But they offer no protection against the sun, which heats them red-hot, nor against the cold wind, which at six thousand feet above sea-level numbs the people at night. These rickety sties, hanging into trees or on to each other, leaning against the mountainside, piled on top of each other, sagging and sliding, are a danger to life. Every time a storm beats its ominous tattoo on the tin roofs, hurling lumps of red clay through the air, as heralds of the tropical rains, the whole neighborhood waits in helpless anxiety to find out whose turn it is now to have his house washed away. Two days earlier, the rain had caused a landslide. One hovel fell with all its inhabitants on top of another hut. They both rolled and slid together, dragging with them two huts hanging farther down the slope. Under the debris, which finally came to a standstill in a stream of mud in the valley, the people found seven dead and twelve wounded persons.

The first raindrops are already falling. Gusts of wind snatch at the tree-tops. Lead-gray clouds suddenly invade the sky. Women begin taking in the washing lying on the roofs to dry. A courteous grocer, with seven rips in his shirt and, with the exception of a sack of manioc, not an ounce of supplies in his "shop", calls us inside. While the rain is falling in sheets and wild music plays on the tin plates of the huts, we dodge from one dry spot to another among the streams of water falling in five places at once through the leaky roof. I think for a moment of the recent landslide, but then I start listening to the parish priest, who is talking about his parish.

The way in which he moves as friend and brother among these poor people makes a deep impression on me. Although he has not been in the parish very long, he knows everyone by name. His only form of apostleship seems to be to live among his people. He must have spent days and weeks moving through these mud quarters.

While I study his intelligent face, I admire the objectivity of his judgment and the sincerity of his social feeling. He is living here in the fifth century. The Romans have departed, and he is one of the leaders of his people. He will do things differently from the way they were done by the white missionaries who founded the Church here in such a surprisingly short time. For, in spite of his European education, he remains a Congolese. He is no organizer or strategist making plans for the future. That is not the African way. But he is a wise man who lives with his people and, case by case, will point the way for the ignorant. I think of Christ's comparing the kingdom of heaven to a piece of leaven. The place where the leaven should be is in the dough and not outside it. It seems to me that this black priest—there are also other types, alas—will like yeast ennoble and sanctify his people. And this was my consolation in the mud quarters of Bukavu.

When after half an hour the rain stopped, the greasy clay surface of the mountain slope was as slippery as glass. It was absolutely impossible to get to the bottom on two legs. From all sides people flocked to help. With axes and picks they dug holes in the tough clay to set our feet in, step by step. Two inhabitants helped me to keep my balance.

When we returned to the priest's house, we were red with clay. We had been three hours on the mountain. Then the car arrived to take us elsewhere. But the forty thousand refugees in Bukavu have to remain where they are. They will go on living as mud-dwellers until the world's conscience awakes.

IN NO-MAN'S-LAND OF KISANGANI

Crammed with tightly-lashed crates and barrels, our C-130 dives out of the burning sky into the tiny circle of free Kisangani. Here freedom has a diameter of six and a quarter miles. Beyond that is the area of the terrible Simbas. At the end of the runway lies a shot-down bomber, which had been forced the day before to make a pancake landing. Our pilot sets his teeth. The cables and electric wiring twisting in and out of the monstrous bowels of the air-compressor seem like an extension of his own nervous system. He has it under iron control. In the nick of time the brakes shriek into action. With an ear-splitting whistle the compressed air finds an outlet somewhere. The safety belt hammers my ribs like a fist. We are lurching dangerously. Groaning with tension, the machine bumps to a stop hardly more than two yards from the wrecked bomber. We have arrived in Kisangani, the former Stanleyville.

Kisangani, once the throbbing heart of the Congo, is now a dead city. The luxuriant municipal gardens have run wild, the shops are closed, the villas are decayed, the population is reduced to half. We are driving around in an oasis that is visibly being swallowed up by the jungle. There is everything to remind us of the dramatic moment when Belgian paratroopers raced against the second-hands of their watches to save the lives of the hostages: on November 24, 1964, they rushed from the airfield to the town along this same route and over the same scorching concrete as we are on now. They saved two thousand lives, but for many they came too late. And certainly too late for the ten to fifteen thousand Congolese who had been killed off like cattle between August and November.

Speechless with horror, we stand before the brickwork where there was once a huge portrait of Lumumba, and where for months the blood of countless human sacrifices flowed over the pavement. We see the hotel Victoria, where the hostages spent their last night before being driven into the street to be shot. We stand on the spot where the Protestant missionary-doctor Paul Carlson was mowed down by a shower of bullets. We see the overgrown gardens where the wounded crawled to find a refuge in which to die alone while they were being searched for elsewhere. In silence we cross the Tshopo Bridge, where the Simbas threw thousands of Congolese into the thundering waterfall of the dam after sewing them into sacks or tying them back-to-back. We stand to pray in the cemetery on the banks of the Congo River, where under silent palm trees and motionless *thuyas* thirty-five martyrs are awaiting the day of their glorious resurrection. They are Belgian, Dutch, Luxembourgian and Spanish nuns and priests, a Protestant clergyman, four Protestant missionaries and a black *abbé*. Then we wander for hours through the military camp, where the stone barracks hum with the voices of thousands of refugees and where the widows and children of the fallen soldiers have found refuge.

This refugee camp is only a mile and a half away from the Simbas. It is estimated that about fifty thousand people are still being held by them in the forest surrounding Stanleyville. Anyone they find with a tin of food or cigarettes is shot down for having had contact with the Americans. The terrorized population lives on nothing but manioc and leaves. Who can count the children who have died of want and exhaustion? Night after night they escape from the forest to get away from terror and misery. Many of the escaped families have lost more than half of their children. The survivors are first taken care of in the hospital. We find a hundred twenty jungle-children there waiting for blood transfusions. In exchange for two bottles of beer the hospital staff find donors among the forced-laborers in yellow and blue prison clothes. They are mostly soldiers who had to choose between death and the Simbas and afterward fell into the hands of the government troops.

Father Balleur, who welcomed his old friend Jan Engelen with tears in his eyes, gave us for these jungle-children some sweets that had arrived in postal packages after the liberation of Kisangani. They had been intended for missionaries of the eastern province, who had meanwhile been killed. The American sweets—from Hempstead, Long Island—so lovingly packed for Sister Mary Antoinette at the mission station of Isangi, bring a gleam of joy to the eyes of twelve-year-old Sophia Kavira, who looks like a child of seven, and to the face of Josephine Assone, who lost six brothers and sisters in the forest. So Sister Mary Antoinette, after her cruel death, still bends with love over the innocent little black children for whom she had lived and died.

For, now that all the unmentionable horrors have passed away and God himself has wiped away her tears of terror and pain, Sister Mary Antoinette knows very well that these black people are no worse than other peoples; that cowardice, egoism and the urge toward self-preservation paralyze all people in their resistance to terror; that the courage to take a stand at the cost of one's own life is as rare among white nations as among colored; that it is not only in the Congo that the masses look on passively while atrocities are being committed; and that this apathy is attributable not so much to wickedness as to fear for one's own skin.

We proceed on farther into no-man's-land between Kisangani and the Simbas. Here lies the Kabondo quarter, called "Brussels". This used to be a very beehive of activity and African life. Eighty to a hundred thousand Congolese used to live here. It is now deserted, being too dangerous. The extensive area is surrounded on three sides by rebels, who at night drag everything they can get out of the houses to make their own lives a little more bearable. In the daytime the Congolese soldiers and the civilian population of Stanleyville take their turns at looting.

The deathly silence is oppressive. There is nothing alive here except the forest, which will soon have swallowed up these forlorn remains of human handiwork. Father Engelen, who knew the pulsing life of "Brussels" in the old days, was more depressed by this scene of desolation than by any other aspect of present-day Congo. The only people we meet are a heavily-armed Katangan patrol and a soldier on a bicycle, who in spite of his ferocious-looking tommy-gun regards us with terror in his eyes. It is a sad excursion past half-demolished houses and cabins whose mud walls lie flat on the ground. Already hidden under rank weeds, rusty carcasses of gutted cars are everywhere to be seen. Standing in the middle of the road is a broken chair. In the untended gardens lie mattresses and cupboards broken open and the contents stolen, which will probably be collected for firewood by the Simbas tonight. In front of a row of houses with windows and doors torn out we see a red-leather armchair in the ditch and a pretty gold-brocade lady's shoe, smeared with blood, lying on top of an empty bird-cage.

As we cannot reach the seminary, which is seven miles from the center of Stan, without risking our lives, we have to be satisfied with a visit to the totally sacked mission of Saint Camille, which is also Kabondo's parish church. Moving through barbed-wire barricades and over a felled tree, we arrive at a group of buildings that were once the spiritual center of this area. Making a path through the wilderness of the garden and the veranda, we reach the deserted house with its gaping doors. All the furniture has been carried away. The floors are covered with papers, torn books and kapok. The electric wiring has been torn from the walls.

We go straight to the closed church. In front of the main entrance lies a "Cheti cha Kualika"—an invitation card, for Zedda

Maurice to take part next Sunday at seven o'clock in the Communion Mass of the League of the Sacred Heart; and on the bulletin board beside the church door hangs a shriveled piece of paper on which, in faded letters, is typed the times of the Masses: "22.11.1964. Today is the 27th Sunday after Pentecost, the last Sunday of the liturgical year. The first Mass will be said for Makaya Joseph, for the intention of his son Kibibi Joseph."

The last Sunday of the liturgical year was also Kabondo's last Sunday. And it was also the last Mass that Kibibi Joseph was able to have said for his deceased father; for the Simbas murdered him on November 24.

That night, under the mosquito-netting in the mission center of Kisangani, I could not sleep. I lay thinking about the future. For after all this desolation comes the day of reconstruction. One thing is certain: that the new mission will have to be humbler and simpler than those that have been destroyed, which were far above the cultural level of these people. There is no longer any use in organizing things on a European level in this primitive country. The Church will have to abandon a great deal and make use only of those things that can be felt by the people as good and useful. Every appearance of luxury must be avoided. No longer any missions like proud castles that give *us* satisfaction but that will always remain strange and meaningless for the Africans. These were discouraging to them and nourished their innate inferiority complex. A cathedral on the mountain-side of Bukavu, where people have to crawl on hands and feet through the mud, is an anomaly estranging the people from the Church. The horror of devastation, which I have seen nowhere so plainly as in the no-man's-land between Kisangani and the Simbas, gives us a new chance. Let us grasp it with both hands by working together with the Congolese to give the Church in this land a shape that is not discouraging but acceptable to these people. Then the sacrifice of so many will not have been in vain.

THE SISTERS OF THE RESURRECTION

The sacrifice of the Congo martyrs has not been in vain. To their intercession I ascribe the prosperous establishment and miraculous rescue of the Resurrection Institute at Bukavu, which has become the finest fruit of my first journey to the Congo.

During the revolt of the white mercenaries, Bukavu was for a time the focal point of world news. This town served as the last headquarters of Major Schramme and his tough band of adventurers. It was here that they won their last battle. It was here that they finally had to surrender to the Congolese army, which, because of American support, had become superior in numbers and weapons. But at the very same time another drama was being enacted, one which the reporters did not bring to the world's attention. It was the ordeal by fire undergone by the Resurrection Institute, affiliated with our relief work, which we had founded together with Mother Hadewych and Father Jan Engelen on November 5, 1966, in Rome.

I had met Mother Hadewych of the Holy Sepulchre in Walungu in 1965, in the midst of the chaos of the Congolese interior. She was a refuge for dozens of young Congolese women who wished to dedicate their lives to God but who did not fit into ordinary religious communities because they had not learned to read and write. It was her opinion, however, that illiteracy ought not to be an obstacle against serving the menaced Church. Had they not as much chance as their more educated sisters of growing in divine love while fulfilling the normal duties of the faithful, and in putting in practice the evangelical counsels? And while living in small communities would they not be able to exercise this love on the lowest steps of spiritual and material-development aid?

Only those who know how deep the gulf already is between the African people and the "évolués", who consider themselves infinitely superior to the masses because they wear a shirt and have a little civilization, can realize how necessary it is to train native development workers who remain in close contact with their people. Therefore, besides teaching-congregations, Africa needs humble and even illiterate nuns with common sense and strong hands. Nuns who are not in the service of a small group of privileged people but of their most primitive fellow-tribesmen who will for many generations form the majority of their people.

It is true that such nuns are of no use for teaching purposes owing to their lack of school learning, which can never be made up for, but they can have other qualities just as indispensable to the Church. Having gone straight to the convent from their parental homes, they have a better knowledge of their people than nuns who have become estranged from their families in the course of their long school training. They remain in contact with their people and can pass over to them the experimental knowledge they have gained in their years of training in religion, catechism, hygiene, and domestic and agrarian matters. In small teams they will be able to serve the outposts. In this way they can become of indispensable assistance to the native priests and a blessing to their country. This was Mother Hadewych's dream. In order to realize this dream, a new institute in the Church had to be founded.

In November 1966, God blessed the undertaking. Mother Hadewych's will-power, Father Engelen's experience, the recommendations of the Archbishop of Bukavu and the broad views of the much-maligned Roman Curia removed all obstacles within seventy-two hours. After three days of intensive work, the new community was established and approved as a papal institute of women bound by vows, who for the love of God place their lives at the service of the menaced Church. This institute is affiliated with the papal work of Aid to the Church in Need and under the authority of the moderator general. The direction of the community during the foundation period is in the hands of Mother Hadewych, assisted by five other nuns of the Holy Sepulchre. When Mother Hadewych flew back to the

Congo, she carried with her the assurance of our financial support and the plans for two houses of the new foundation.

She did not allow the grass to grow under her feet. She began at once with the purchase of a truck and building materials. An Italian planter, Franco Micheletti, was given charge of the building work. The postulants' house rose at the edge of a morass at Miranga in the parish of Ciherano. The novitiate was built in record time in Bukavu on a small, paradisiacal peninsula next to a Jesuit retreat house also being built, where the novices will do the household chores.

When everything was almost ready and the furniture for the two houses had already been bought, the conflict broke out between the Congolese government and Schramme's mercenaries. Bukavu stood in the front line. For a month the nuns were in danger of their lives. On August 18, 1967, Mother Hadewych wrote from Rwanda: "We have been through a great deal these last few weeks: shooting, murdering, stealing, until it became impossible to stay at Bukavu. The bishop ordered us to evacuate. We are therefore refugees and have to leave everything behind. We used the truck to escape, and the exhausted driver drove us into a ravine. One of the novices is in the hospital. They want to send us back to Belgium. We have refused. We are here with four novices, four postulants and four white sisters. The candidates are in Walungu or have returned for the time being to their families. We are fools for God and now really belong to the Church in distress, but we are keeping up our spirits. If it depends on sacrifices and crosses we shall have a splendid resurrection!"

While the almost completed convents at Bukavu and Miranga were being sacked and stripped of their doors, windows and roofs, Mother Hadewych continued her way of the cross. She was sent from one town to the other and finally driven from Rwanda to Burundi. The cross was God's seal on the foundation charter of the young community. For what else could be expected after the miraculously smooth negotiations in Rome than that the Institute of the Resurrection would have to be marked with the sign of the suffering Christ? This distinction was granted when the whole of the work collapsed in the storm of the mercenaries' revolt. Mother Hadewych was the last to leave Bukavu, and she was the first to return, in spite of the hatred in the triumphant Congolese army of everything that was European. She returned to a heap of rubble.

When about six months after her return I flew back to the Congo for a short visit, I was able to spend the night in the little convent at Bukavu—for the most part restored and half-habitable. To write about it is easy, but the superhuman efforts that this restoration cost can be read only in the wrinkles in Mother Hadewych's face, which in one year's time became ten years older. The kingdom of heaven had suffered violence, but the suffering had borne fruit. With amazement I learned that all the candidates and postulants had returned as soon as the news had spread that Mother Hadewych was back in Bukavu. They had walked for two, three or even four days to get there. The last of them came from Rwanda, almost two hundred miles away, and had to cross the border clandestinely to follow their vocation.

In the meantime, the first nuns have made their temporary vows. Together with the novices and a number of postulants, they are now busy completing the building. They pray and cook; and at the consecration of their daily Mass, they beat the tom-tom in their spartan chapel. Sister Siarda and Sister Lucas are guiding the novices' first steps along the rough road of spiritual life. In a noble effort the novices are straining to control their wild nature. But when the watchdogs bark at night, they spring up from their mattresses and run undaunted through the building site in their white nightdresses and fluttering coifs. They terrify the thieves who come practically every night in rowboats across Lake Kivu to steal building materials. They captured one boat with its three thieves, all paralyzed with fear, thinking the novices were ghosts, and delivered them over to the police.

We also visited Miranga. There we found on a wooded height the deserted settlement of the gold-seekers, where three nuns and forty-two candidates are temporarily living. Surrounding a ramshackle house are a number of small stables scattered in the woods. In each stable sleep six candidates. They have each at their disposal half a mattress and a nail in the wall on which they can hang their clothes and other poor possessions. Under a penthouse roof, a pan of beans and a mush of tapioca flour are simmering on the open fire. Together with dried fish, this is the daily menu in the Institute of the Resurrection. There is another shed in which a priest from the neighboring mission station celebrates Mass daily and where the candidates receive their lessons.

Sisters Ursula, Elfrieda and Caritas of the Holy Sepulchre live in the centrally situated house, which must at one time have looked like a kind of villa but now, with its crumbling walls and rotting planks, is more like a picturesque ruin. The room that used to be the drawing room is now the chapel. In the kitchen, which is at the same time the living room, sewing room and storeroom, there are a table and a couple of chairs next to the brick oven. Goatherds often spend the night in the adjacent stable. In the evening they play their stringed instruments near a wood fire and hum monotonous songs while the nuns in the kitchen are trying to pray their Office by the light of a kerosene lamp. Cedars, eucalyptus trees and slender gravileas stand on guard around this convent, whose bitter poverty reminds me of the life of the ancient desert fathers. Does not this poverty counterbalance in a supernatural way the love of ease, repulsion to sacrifice and overhumanizing tendency that are poisoning the Church at the present time?

Past tea plantations and cinchona groves we reach the morass that lies a mile and a half away. The Mwami granted some eighteen acres of this area to the sisters. The candidates are reclaiming the land under the direction of Sister Ursula, who has enthusiastically returned in her old age to the farming skills she knew in her youth. It is almost incomprehensible that uneducated girls with the most primitive of means have succeeded in such a short time, by means of an irrigation system, in turning part of the desert into fertile, arable land. Carrots, cabbages, sweet potatoes and crimson tomatoes, arousing the admiration of the whole population, have been conjured out of the ground in a few months' time. This is the same kind of civilizing work done by the monks in Europe in earlier times, with this difference: that these girls have not even the wherewithal to provide themselves with an ox and a plow.

At the edge of the newly dug field stands the first wing of the almost-completed little convent that the sisters will have to move into even before the beginning of the rainy season. Half of the roof is still uncovered because the roofing material was stolen. They are waiting also for cement, which is three months overdue. Franco Micheletti, who escaped death by a miracle and has at long last turned up again after he had been in hiding for weeks at a time in a cellar, shows with justifiable pride the plans for the little cottages that are each to hold ten candidates. He will begin to build as soon as the money and the cement have arrived. He has promised me not to return to Italy, where his wife and children are waiting for him, until all the buildings are finished. He is sixty-three years old.

Before I take my departure, we make up an inventory of everything that these pioneers of the Resurrection are still in need of. It is a long list, on which there is room for the dinner service, the school desks, working-shoes, spare clothing and the plow, as well as the draft-ox and the fifty rosaries, which are indispensable for the spiritual and material progress of this enterprise. Is it difficult to understand that before leaving I have given Mother Hadewych carte blanche to purchase everything she needs, at our expense?

Since then, it has been raining bills that we could not possibly pay without extra help. So in December 1968 I wrote to my benefactors: "What about an extra Christmas gift for the Sisters of the Resurrection who are still living in stables in Miranga? The Child who was born in a stable will be grateful to you. And the old ass Werenfried, who always promises more than he has got, will not feel so lonely near the manger if you do not forget the ox, which costs only 100 dollars and which he is going to send to Mother Hadewych after Christmas."

Within a month I received sufficient money for a herd of quite two thousand oxen. A retired teacher in Germany gave the whole of her savings of a hundred thousand deutsche marks for the completion of Miranga. And a girl who gave up her vacation money began her letter by naïvely writing: "Dear ass Werenfried"!

This poor ass, who in 1953 founded the Building Companions and in 1956 the Secular Institute of Building Brethren, and who in 1960 lost both foundations together with a great many of his illusions, was determined not to stumble twice against the same stone and not to found any more institutes. Now that God has decided otherwise, he takes courage from the consideration that the Resurrection Institute was born of the blood of the Congolese martyrs and that it is supported by the love of innumerable faithful benefactors. I look forward to the future with great hope because I have met in this Institute people of prayer and spiritual life who are not turned from their purpose by any affliction. Perhaps they are living in a spiritual night. They are afflicted like Job and have repeatedly lost all they have. But in God they find the strength to begin over and over again. Their spirit of total abnegation was a precious lesson to me. Their sense of humor was a help to me. This sense of humor saves them just as much from overestimation of themselves as from despair. It springs from the insight that the world is in God's hand and that not a hair of their heads will be harmed against his will.

In this spirit I have for the third time in my life ventured to found a spiritual community, knowing that the future does not depend on us, but on Almighty God, whose useless servants we are.

A young Christian in Chad.

The nuns are indispensable in Bukavu.

Daughters of the Resurrection, Bukavu.

Dispensing medicine in Bukavu.

Daughters of the Resurrection and the people of Mumumbano.

A woman with child working in the fields near Bukavu.

Behind the Iron Curtain

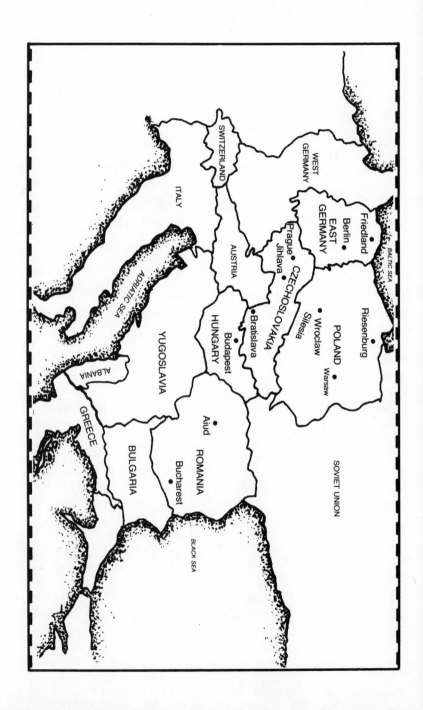

THE CURTAIN IS STILL THERE

When Jesus died on the Cross, the sky was darkened, the earth quaked and the curtain of the Temple was rent in twain. Since that time, many have been crucified. Time and again the princes of this world have conspired against God and his Anointed. Herod, Beria, Caiaphas, Hitler, Pilate, Stalin, Khrushchev. Their time is past, and they were wafted away like chaff before the wind, when the measure of their wickedness was full.

But after Pilate came Nero, after Caiaphas came Alexis and after Khrushchev came Mao. Thus Good Friday always comes around again, and the crosses stand in their thousands above scaffolds and gas-chambers and above the mass graves of those who died of a shot in the neck.

Good Friday and the cross have remained; and the curtain is there, too, to hide the blood-thirstiness of the murderers. Oh, don't call them Marshal or Your Excellency when they come to visit you with gloves on and a smile. Remember that the glove covers the claws of a thug, and that behind the smile they are planning murder. Their hands are stained with the blood of Jesus. Call them murderers. Call your children back from the street-corners where those murderers will be passing and bolt your doors as long as they are in your city. Call them murderers and don't be deceived by the curtain. For they have made an iron curtain of it, so strong and indivisible that no justice can pierce it. Don't therefore wait for the curtain to be rent, as did the children of Jerusalem, before lamenting the death of the innocent. The curtain will not be rent until the vials of suffering are full. But behind the curtain, Judas is counting his pieces of silver and the witnesses are giving false witness. And weeping behind the curtain, Jerusalem has intoned the Lamentations of Jeremiah. There they are chasing the Bandit of Nazareth with sticks and swords. Like Peter, most of the faithful have become afraid and fainthearted. Like Mary, the mothers are weeping for their captive children. The priests are being satiated with hyssop and vinegar. And, with Jesus, the Church is hanging on the Cross and dying. And still the curtain, the Iron Curtain, is hanging unrent across God's temple, dividing holy Church. For the days of affliction have not yet been fulfilled.

Good Friday has still not come to an end. From Christ it extends to Stephen, James, Peter and Paul, Clement, Ignatius of Antioch, Cosmas and Damian and all the martyrs up to Cardinal Stepinac († 1960) and the Ukrainian bishops Chomysyn († Kiev, 1945), Kocylowskyj († 1947), Romza († Mukavic, 1947), Budka († Karaganda, 1948), Hopko (arrested and disappeared without trace, 1950), Lakota († Workuta, 1950), Latysevakyj († Siberia, 1957), Werhun († Angarsk, 1957), Czarneckyj († Siberia, 1959), Gojdyc († Lwow, 1960) and countless others who are still being martyred and crucified for the sake of the kingdom of heaven. For the Master himself formulated the constitution of Christendom: he decreed that the Christ must suffer all this in order to enter into his glory.

This law is now being fulfilled by the Church behind the Curtain, by our brothers and sisters who were required to deliver their bodies, souls and hearts to Jesus, so that suffering and dying in their humanity he might make up for what is still lacking in redemption.

It is still Good Friday with its agony, hatred, human failure, ridicule, maltreatment, ingratitude, the inexpressible sorrow, the bitter way of the Cross, the crucifixion and shameful death of our Lord, Jesus Christ. Now no longer in his own blessed body, but in those who by grace share his life and who are his members.

The Curtain is still there, behind which Christ is carrying the Cross to Calvary. Utterly forsaken, he is driven forward and dragged to the place of execution. Exhausted, he sinks under the spiritual and physical burden that he has to bear. His intelligence and will, they have broken with devilish arts and secret herbs. They have made him like one insane, one mechanically repeating what they whisper in his ear.

It is no man but a worm who is crawling up Mount Calvary. There is not a friend to support him—they have all been deported to Siberia or to the uranium mines. Now they are tearing the garments from his body. Now the hammer blows are thudding through all the fibers of his tortured body. Now he is hanging on the Cross. "I thirst", he says, and "God, my God, why hast thou forsaken me?"

It is still Good Friday. Bloody Friday of the Church in distress. All that remains is the task once fulfilled by the Angel of Consolation on the Mount of Olives; by the weeping women of Jerusalem; by Veronica, who wiped Jesus' face; by Simon, who helped him bear his Cross; by his Mother, who stayed with him till all was consummated.

To continue these offices of mercy by a glance of encouragement, by a crust of bread or a refreshing drink, by pouring oil and wine in the smarting wounds . . . to continue this high act of charity behind the Curtain—this is our debt of honor to the persecuted Church which is Christ.

PEACEFUL COEXISTENCE?

Our relief work for the persecuted Church is impeded not so much by the Communists as by Catholics who at each smile or tactical concession of the Red rulers believe that the end of the persecution has arrived. They are poisoned by the slogan of "peaceful coexistence". Since the day when this expression was invented by the wily Khrushchev, they have underestimated the mortal danger of Communism and flirted with dubious peace movements, with progressive conceptions and with the wolves in sheep's clothing who have entered the fold of the Church.

It seems to us not impossible that this so-called progressiveness is partly the result of fear and the love of ease. A practical materialism is now spreading more and more in the Church, bringing with it a reluctance to make sacrifices. There is a growing lack of fighting spirit and especially of courage to combat oneself and voluntarily take upon oneself the hardships demanded of us at this turning-point of world history. Many champions of peaceful coexistence show a strong resemblance to Christian Communist fellow-travelers endeavoring to save their own peace and standard of life by means of a compromise with the rulers of tomorrow. Of course, their consciences have to be salved. So the inherent evil of Communism is minimized and reports of Communist moral constraint are set aside as exaggerated and fanatical. For this reason they are endeavoring in the name of coexistence and in the interests of peace (which is no peace), to turn the Church of the free world into a silent Church, too. At the same time they are disseminating diligently the theory that Communism has developed and altered.

This theory is false. It is quite a wrong idea that convinced Communists desire to make peace with God and are prepared to give the Church her freedom. Those who declare that conditions have essentially improved for the menaced Church in Communist-ruled countries are mistaken.

In Yugoslavia or in Czechoslovakia during the "Prague spring", where the position of the Church had undergone some temporary improvement, there is or was no question of an authentic Communist regime. That is why Moscow is doing everything it can to restore the status quo ante. In the Communist countries under Russian hegemony, nothing has changed. Freedom of religious instruction is still greatly curtailed. Control of church attendance and the punitive measures against practicing Catholics have not been canceled. The "separation" of Church and State is a farce. The interference of party and government in purely ecclesiastical fields of government and jurisdiction has not come to an end. The training of new priests has been reduced to a minimum or quite abolished. The parents have been deprived of the right to educate their children. Compulsory atheistic education is unavoidable. The scandal of the puppet pastors and Quisling prelates forced upon the Church is still undiminished.

In this religious persecution we are not concerned with how many pints of blood have been shed but with the systematic strangling of all the organs essential to the Church and with the total eradication of all forms of worship. This is being done so thoroughly, so deliberately and with such irresistible logic that we are compelled to ascribe this unprecedented revolt against God to a supernatural cause. As an East-European Council-father expressed it, we may call Communism a "collective possession by the devil".

There were about sixty bishops of the persecuted Church present at the Second Vatican Council. Most of them lived under an inhuman pressure. I have seen bishops huddled together like frightened birds, afraid of any conversation and of the "guides" sent with them as secretaries by the government. They did not open their mouths, but their silence was a shattering indictment. Our silence would be treachery. This truth has been confirmed by many of them. They have implored me to go on preaching the passion of the persecuted Church. They have assured me that their desperate church people would not understand it if we ceased to denounce Communism. They have beseeched me to combat the dangerous phantasm of a compromise with the devil.

The present-day tactics of the persecutors are aimed at sparing the shepherds and destroying the flock. Cardinals Slipyi and Beran, Bishop Schubert, Monsignor Menges and a few others were, as a matter of fact, released and pushed off to the West. But these liberated bishops are no proof of the freedom of the Church. As long as they are prevented from returning to their dioceses and from exercising their episcopal functions, they are living in exile, their freedom is Communist guile and the Church is as much oppressed as she ever was.

It is no doubt possible that Communism has now its reasons for a more moderate policy with regard to the Church. It would not be justifiable to exclude this possibility. But it would be equally unjustifiable lightheartedly to forget the Communists' ruthlessness during half a century and to negotiate with them as normal partners. After all, the ecclesiastical negotiators have been deceived by them; let us not judge them by their words but by their deeds. And these deeds are still immutably directed toward the total destruction of the Church. As long as no apparent change has been made in this objective, the Church cannot possibly conclude a pact with Moscow without losing the trust of the persecuted. And the persecuted people's trust in us is more precious than a *modus vivendi* with the oppressors. This is proved by the experience of the nineteenth century.

We are not opposed to a conversation with Moscow if it is carried on by competent people. But it would be false on our part to prepare for such a conversation by hushing up the religious persecution. This would be shooting our brothers in the back. Only the truth can set us free.

Among other things, the truth appears from the history of the Orthodox Church in the Soviet Union. It is the history of a Church successively struck, deceived, incarcerated, ridiculed and made to serve Communism. After multitudes of its faithful, priests and bishops had sealed their loyalty to Christ with their blood, one weakling was found prepared to make concessions. He was the first of the prelates who have become the servants of the Communists. He honored Stalin as a wise leader whom God himself had placed at the head of the Russian people. He organized collections to provide airplanes and tanks for the Red Army. He was silent about the persecution. While Communist wolves were mangling his own sheep, he assisted them by the extermination of the Ukrainian Uniate Church. And while the Slavic peoples of Eastern Europe were sighing under Soviet terror, he wrote in a pastoral letter: "The Vatican is the center of fascism and of the international conspiracy against the Slavic peoples. It is one of the instigators of two imperialistic wars and is now playing an active part in unchaining a new war against world democracy."

Later utterances cause us to suspect that Patriarch Alexis, who, moreover, was specifically condemned by Pope Pius XII, did not write this libelous accusation through wickedness but through weakness. Yet great caution should be exercised in all dealings with him and with his collaborators. These henchmen of Communism have made the Russian Church far more subservient to the State than it ever was in the time of the Czars. It is a mistake to consider them the undisputed leaders of Orthodoxy. The true Orthodox Church, which has remained true to Christ, does not acknowledge him. It declines any compromise with atheism. It is being violated in the penal institutions of Siberia. Its priests are imprisoned, degraded to the rank of unskilled laborers, or live like vagrants for God. Instead of Communist medals, they wear the calumny and shame of the Man of Sorrows. The legitimate Orthodox Church has withdrawn into holy illegality. Although in the last few years thousands of churches and almost all the priest seminaries of the Soviet Union have been closed, it is still surviving in a holy and spiritual way in the catacombs. It has more right to our interest and sympathy than do the prelates who have sold themselves to Moscow and consider themselves the official mouthpieces of Orthodoxy.

We are not against ecumenism. Our ecumenical achievements consist in the brotherly help we have for years been giving to the persecuted Orthodox Christians, and also in our prayers for the Orthodox collaborators, that God may cure them of their blindness.

There is much spiritual confusion. While we are talking of the reunion of churches, our inner unity is being threatened. The Catholic Church is being rent. The doctrinal and disciplinary crisis is so severe that many a bishop is no longer master of the situation. Over-hasty reformers are already condemning the pre-Johannine Church. Thus a pope who died for peace and unity is now being annexed by one group and misused as a principle of discord. This discord is being fomented by Moscow. That is why, in 1963, *Pravda* published this: "There are at the moment only two great statesmen: Khrushchev, who achieved de-Stalinization, and Pope John, who initiated de-Pacellization." Many Catholics have swallowed this poison. By setting John up against Pius, they set Christ up against Christ, instead of setting up Christ against a world with which he has never wished to be reconciled.

In this way Pope John's goodness was falsely interpreted. Thus the theory that collaboration with Communism is desirable was distilled from *Pacem in terris*, although this idea is to be found neither in the letter nor in the spirit of the encyclical.

We have been reproached for calling Communism a devilish system. We do so because this ideology is inspired by hatred of God and is wicked in its deepest core. We believe in the existence of the devil. He is the tireless ambusher of the Church. The same Satan who once possessed Judas is now able to subject to himself people, organizations and worldwide movements in order to continue his implacable struggle against God. Isn't Lucifer's proud claim of founding a paradise on earth without God recognizable in Communism? And has this system not told sufficient lies to justify the fear that it is possessed by the Father of All Lies? And should his terrifying successes not be ascribed to a satanic mind?

We are not advocates of a crusade against Communism. Christ was a lover of peace. He sat at table with sinners and did not refuse Judas' kiss. That is why Pope John XXIII considered it un-Christian to refuse the handshake of a Communist. Even if Communists are the servants of Satan, they have a right to expect us to return good for evil. If they slap us in the face, they may expect, in virtue of the Gospel, that we should turn the other cheek. We owe them a Christian answer because they can recover the God they have lost only by the manifestation of authentic Christianity.

It is tragic that they themselves are preventing this manifestation. Where they are in power, the Church dies. In their territories, Christ may not be preached to the young. They are destroying families. In their people's republics, they are forcing the mothers to do men's work and the children into "social institutes", where they learn to hate God. "It would be better if they had never been born", wrote a Slovakian mother of her four children, who are being brought up in Communist boarding schools. Bishops and priests whom the Communists release from dungeons are condemned to silence, so that their freedom is false. They are thwarting Christ's sacred command to teach all peoples and instruct them to keep all the commandments he has given. In this way they themselves have quenched God's light and smothered God's voice, so that, according to Isaiah's terrible word, they are in danger of being those who "having eyes yet . . . do not see, and having ears do not hear, and having hearts do not understand", so that they cannot be converted to God and be healed by him.

This should fill us with great concern. They are God's people, and the Light that has come into the world wants to shine also in their darkness. This is possible only if we ourselves give new life to true Christianity, which they have condemned to death behind their Iron Curtain. It must radiate warmth to them at every encounter. Tourists and business people ought to carry it to the East.

Everywhere in the Red East, intellectuals and artists are fascinated by the ideal of freedom. An irrepressible spiritual revolt against Communism has broken loose. The possibility is becoming clear that God needs no war at all to destroy this system in an apocalyptic manner. He is probably better served if this shame collapses from within; when nature resumes its rights; when the builders of the Red empire themselves recognize that their paradise has become a hell, in which they are being tormented by fear, despair, distrust, terror and hate, so that they themselves destroy the work of their own hands. This process has already begun. The revolution of the young Communists, who have unmasked Communism as deceit, is on its way.

As God has no right to speak under the atheistic regime and

has therefore disappeared from the consciousness of many, this revolution is being inspired less by religious than by humanistic ideas. Yet in large segments of society a spontaneous trust in the Catholic Church is still living, the latter having taken the most courageous stand against oppression. An eleventh-hour cooperation with Communism would kill this trust.

The future of the Church is not safe with collaborators. The feeble shepherds and "peace priests" who have taken service, for whatever reason, with the oppressor are harvesting hatred and contempt. The trust of the oppressed is with the intransigent figures, who have fearlessly denounced the sin of Communism, though in all love for the sinners, and have consistently refused to betray the poor for the sake of temporary gain.

The Church of the nineteenth century is reproached with having identified herself too much with the ruling classes and was too late in acknowledging the legitimate claims of the exploited proletariat. In this way she lost the confidence of the poor. Now, however, behind the Iron Curtain she has regained this confidence because she has steadfastly refused to be reconciled with a system that treads underfoot the rights of man just as much as capitalism does.

It is obvious that the growing sympathy for Rome is an obstacle to the antireligious action of the Communists. Something has to be done about it. As it is now not opportune for them to make martyrs, they are trying to transfer the tiresome symbols of ecclesiastical resistance to the West. It is to their advantage if Mindszenty, Beran and Slipyi leave the people's republics. This gives them propaganda opportunities to represent these martyrs as deserters and to play off the feeling of forsaken discouragement among the abandoned faithful against the Church. On the other hand, by humanizing their anti-Church measures they wish to suggest that these measures have been suspended. This is misleading. Humanly speaking, the released bishops are better off than they were; but they are not free bishops. To the Church it makes absolutely no difference whether a bishop is prevented from ruling his diocese by a prison wall, by a wrought-iron garden gate or by exile to Rome.

We must not allow ourselves to be misled. All seeming concessions and all rumors about a less-severe attitude of Communism toward the Church are in reality only cunning means to break down the Church's power of resistance and lead her to a slow capitulation, to deprive her of the faith of the poor and to restore the authority of the Communist leaders.

In reality the condition of the persecuted Church is still deteriorating. With sorrow and anger in our hearts, we ascertain that the Communist oppressors are succeeding more and more in making a wilderness of the last remains of the earthly paradise in which the Creator could still walk undisturbed. As they never succeed in winning inwardly-full-grown and normally-thinking people permanently for their tyranny, they are making a huge effort to contaminate by violence and cunning millions of defenseless children and to misuse them in the service of their system.

God is the friend of these little ones. The emotion aroused in us when we catch a glimpse of a lost paradise in their eyes is only a faint reflection of what goes on in the mind of the Lord when he sees the purity of his own Being reproduced in their immaculate souls. They are as fresh as spring flowers and as pure as the morning dew. In them he is well pleased.

That is why we may not forbid the children—to whom the kingdom of heaven belongs—from coming to him. And the strongest expression of tenderness that has come down to us from the Master is in regard to the unknown child whom "he enfolded in his arms" (Mk 9:36). His love for that child was so immeasurable that he identified himself with him in the astounding assurance: "Whosoever shall receive one of these little children in my name, receives me." In regard to the children, he commands us therefore to have the same respect, care and love for them as we owe to him. In this way he wants to preserve his inalienable property from all evil and be himself the guarantee that no harm shall come to them. And foreseeing what would be done to his protégés by ruthless corrupters, he hurled into the world the horrifying threat: "And whoso shall offend one of these little ones who believe in me, it is better for him if a millstone were hung about his neck and he were cast into the sea." Facts justify the fear that this curse is applicable to the ideologists of Communism, who are systematically and with fiendish cunning estranging millions of innocent children from God and training them to be against him.

It is time there came an end to the minimizing of this danger. The Soviet educational system, in proud battle-array against the Most High, a system that is deliberately accepted and put into practice throughout the whole Communist world, should be an eye-opener. While men are dreaming of peace and conciliation with those who raise themselves against God, the devil is working feverishly at the total demolition of God's kingdom in the hearts of the little ones. The Lord will curse us if by our silence we become accessories to this crime. He cannot possibly resign himself to peaceful coexistence that involves the loss to him of all youths.

The Church can renounce earthly possessions. To prevent greater harm she can in silence allow herself to be deprived of earthly rights. In the realization of the guilt and sin of her children, she can humble herself before despots whose hands are stained with the blood of millions: she acknowledges in them the scourge of a wrathful God and bends weeping beneath his chastising hand. But never can she gamble away the inviolable rights of eternal God at the conference table. Never can she accept to do merely what the rebels-against-God graciously permit. For she has herself her own divine driving-power, which God himself laid down in his ineluctable commandment that mankind shall serve him with all its heart, with all its soul and with all its strength. This commandment to the Church must be made known to every living person, and each generation must be taught to fulfill it. This duty may not be set aside for the sake of a false peace. The Church remains the Mother and Mistress of God's own children, to whom she has given birth, not for the world with its transient countenance, but for eternity, in which God himself will dry all tears and avenge all wrongs. May eternal God help the Church to remain steadfast in the fight that she may not shirk.

CROSSES ON WHICH OUR BROTHERS ARE HANGING

During Passiontide in the churches, the crosses are veiled, but everywhere in the wide world they are being used to torture and to kill—crosses on which our brothers are dying. And in these brothers Christ is dying. . . .

I met Cardinal Wyszynski in 1956. He was not in prison. He was not handcuffed, but he was being spiritually crucified. He was suffering under the responsibility of having had to say *no* to the Polish government, thereby himself giving the signal for further difficulties. He knew the risk he ran. He knew which of his priests were likely to become weak and cowardly. He could estimate the percentage of apostates. He was tormented by anxiety about what was going to happen, by doubt as to whether he would not have done better to make some concessions, by the sorrow in which so many would be plunged. Jesus is risen from the dead, but the hordes of his enemies would march on Good Friday to the lonely cardinal. "Whom do you seek", he would ask. "Jesus of Nazareth", they would reply. "That am I." Yes, that was he, the cardinal with the face of a diplomat. A few years before, he was still the diplomat, to the greatest limit of what was permissible in his breathtaking game with Gomulka. Now he was the lonely Wyszynski, in whom Christ suffered on the cross in Warsaw.

And Cardinal Mindszenty. I still feel my hands in his on that All Saints' Day in Budapest, when I was with him three hours after his liberation. Four days later he had to flee like hunted game to the American Embassy, where for many long years he had to watch the death-struggle of the Hungarian Church.

This resolute man, who before the war was called the Red Prelate on account of his progressive social ideas and who was now being reviled by Communists and progressive Catholics as a reactionary, baroque bishop, this misunderstood, scorned and calumniated cardinal was crucified for Jesus Christ's sake. His cross was finely polished, and his dungeon was fitted with all modern conveniences, but he was powerless. In spite of his vehement temperament he could not defend himself. He could do nothing to relieve the immeasurable suffering of his people. He was under censorship—for even the letters sent him by diplomatic mail-bag were returned if they contained information about religious persecution. His cross stood in the American Embassy at Budapest.

Another cross was being borne by Dr. Hieronymous Menges. After the apostolic administrator of Bucharest was sentenced to fifty years' imprisonment, Dr. Menges became his successor. Almost at once the Romanian government demanded of him that he separate himself from Rome. When he refused, he was accused of espionage. He was taken from his bed at dead of night and thrown, handcuffed, into prison. To force him to make false admissions, he was fetched from his cell three or four times a night and beaten. A man he had never seen in his life testified that he had been repeatedly ordered to post letters for him addressed to the pope. Later on Menges was locked in a cell and made to walk up and down day and night. Whenever he rested for a moment, the jailer struck him in the face—till he had no more teeth in his mouth. After a day and a half, he collapsed. For days he lay on a plank bed, seriously ill. Suffering from suppuration of the nose cavity, he was not allowed a handkerchief. The newspaper he used instead of a handkerchief was taken away. For twelve years he suffered like this in twenty-four prisons. On August 1, 1964, he was made to take off his striped prison clothes and walk naked across a courtyard to another building. There lay a heap of rags from which he might choose some clothing. Dressed in a pair of trousers too large for him, a faded jacket and no shirt or underwear, he was released. For seventeen months he lived poor and sick in Romania. Then he was pushed off to the West as a *Volksdeutscher* (person of German descent). But he brought the cross of his bitter memories and of his helplessness back with him to Germany.

The cross that so many have to bear is the mental pressure of persecution. Anxiety and distrust are like infectious diseases affecting everyone. Some people become insane. It has repeatedly happened that priests have committed suicide. A few years ago it happened in Czechoslovakia that a priest broke off his Mass just before the consecration, sat down on the altar steps and, weeping bitterly, tore the pages out of the Mass book. He was shut up in an asylum. The metal worker who is also his bishop declares that the priest collapsed under the moral conflict of the silent Church: either to administer the sacraments at the expense of truth or to preach the Gospel at the expense of the sacraments. For those who preach the truth are suspended from the priesthood; and those who wish to continue administering the sacraments must renounce preaching the truth.

In this way one priest after another is sentenced to prison or to a neutral existence in a kind of asylum for old and dying Christians. He can choose between a labor camp and a museum, but he must leave the young alone. This makes him a man without a future, a soldier at a deserted post. All that he can do is either die or capitulate. A good many lose their courage and their minds in this spiritual night, on which no daylight seems to fall. How many of our brothers have already died on this cross?

Joan Tautu is another who has died. He was a Greek-Catholic priest in Romania and married to a teacher named Silvia. They loved each other and were happy in the service of the Lord and in the privacy of their young family. But in 1947 their happiness came to an end after three and a half years of marriage when Tautu was sentenced for his Faith's sake to ten years' imprisonment.

One cold November night he was made to leave his parish, Silvia and his two-year-old daughter, Anina. For ten long years he heard nothing from his bishop, who had been murdered, and nothing from the two persons whom he loved. But he bore humiliation, tortures and hardships in steadfast loyalty, in the hope of seeing Silvia and Anina again. For ten long years he had to be silent about God. For ten long years he could speak to his fellow-prisoners only about his daughter and about Silvia's last birthday, when he had surprised her with the book called *The Lord's Tunic*. She had then been so happy that her eyes had shone in a way that he had never seen in anyone else. Together with God's presence in his heart, the light in her eyes and the way she had looked at him had remained with him during those ten years in the lead mines of Baia Sprie.

Then came the day of freedom. It was on Christmas eve, 1957. Released from prison, Tautu left with his bundle under his arm, in the rags he had worn for ten years and wearing heavy shoes soon drenched with snow and water. First he visited a ruined church to thank God for helping him to persevere and because he would soon now be able to embrace Silvia and Anina. For him, time had stood still in 1947, and he lived in the conviction that his dear ones would still be as he had left them, that time had not touched them and that the light in Silvia's eyes would still be as bright as on her last birthday. On his journey home, it seemed to him that time and the train were standing still and that he would never get there.

Late in the evening he at last reached his home town. He had made up his mind first to change his clothes and then to go with Silvia and Anina to Midnight Mass. He took a detour so that none of his parishioners would see how poorly dressed he was. There was his house! His heart beat in his throat when he peered through the lighted kitchen window. But what he saw was not his, not his furniture, nothing that he recognized. Beside the stove somebody was sitting on a chest, elbows on knees and head in hands. The house must have been expropriated, and Silvia must have gone away.

Joan Tautu knocked on the window to ask where Silvia was. An aged woman stood up slowly. Her back was bent, her hair was white and she had a wrinkled face. Tautu asked for Silvia and explained that he was the former owner of the house. The woman invited him to come in, looked at him searchingly and touched his face with her calloused hands as if he were a ghost: "Is it you, Joan? Are you alive? Is it really you?" The brilliant light of her eyes had vanished. His ten-year-old dream was over. He found a Silvia broken by suffering. In the only room the state had allowed her, there was nothing to eat and not a trace of festivity. It was a new prison with the same misery and the same hardships as in Baia Sprie.

Silvia went to borrow some food from neighbors. Then the two ate in silence. Afterward Silvia told him that after his arrest she had been dismissed as a school teacher and that she now did washing for the new masters of the town; and that in 1947 she had taken Anina to her parents' remote village. In the whole of the ten years she had seen her daughter only twice! For Tautu this was the bitterest Christmas of his life. In prison he had lived on hope, but the reality had taken all his hope away.

On the third day after Christmas, he went into the woods as a woodsman. This was the work that had been assigned him. He lived on bread and bacon and worked from the morning till the evening as hard as he could in order to earn a little more than the usual wages, so as to begin a new life and to have Anina at home again. For three months he toiled in the woods and was able now and again to buy something for the house or some clothes for Silvia. But one night he came home so exhausted from work that he did not even wake up when Silvia opened the door to the secret police. They had come to fetch Tautu again, for the prosecutor had appealed against his release and demanded another five years' imprisonment for him.

Joan Tautu had to leave Silvia behind again. Without having celebrated the liturgy even once and without having seen Anina, he was sent to the prison in Jilava, a subterranean dungeon into which no light ever penetrates, a man broken in mind and body.

In 1961, I learned that he suffered from tuberculosis in the lungs and bones. If he had been released, he never could have worked as a woodsman to save Silvia and Anina. He also has borne an unbearably heavy cross.

In Hong Kong stands Bishop Bianchi's cross. I have eaten and drunk with him. He does not talk about the past. He seems to be an ordinary bishop. But Hong Kong is only a small part of his diocese. The remainder lies in Red China. He was for years a prisoner there. He was tortured, beaten and humiliated. He ended up as a menial worker and was finally driven out of the country with cudgels. When the British border-guard asked who he was, he said he was bishop of Hong Kong. He might just as well have called himself the emperor of China. They arrested him at the border because they thought he was mad. He was released only when a priest whom he had himself ordained fell weeping on his knees before him because he recognized in this maltreated menial worker his own bishop.

Bishop Bianchi was a bishop like so many others. But what was he thinking when with every convoy of refugees he heard bad news of his diocese, his priests, his nuns, his faithful? In Hong Kong stands the cross on which he slowly died.

What follows now is the way of the cross of a nuns' convent in Latvia. There were originally thirty-two sisters who devoted themselves to the sick in the city and the district. They were loved throughout the whole area for their devotion and readiness to help. When Latvia was occupied by the Russians in 1939, a wave of terror spread over the country. The nuns were expelled from their convent and had to leave their hospital. All except Sister Laetitia and Sister Teresita fled to Poland. These two, dressed as peasants, went into hiding in a neighboring village. Now and again they came to the city to see what was happening to the convent and to the hospital. Crucifixes, books and all other religious objects had been thrown out of the windows on to the street, carted off in vans to the dump and there burned.

Their hospital became a military hospital. After six months, the Russians discovered that the two peasant girls who sometimes came to the city were nuns from what had once been the convent. They were arrested, placed against the hospital wall and shot.

In 1941, when Latvia was taken by the Germans, the other nuns were allowed to return, but it was not a real liberation. The difficulties remained very grave. Of the original thirty-two nuns, there were still nineteen left. The convent had suffered heavy damage. The hospital remained in military hands. After a year, the nuns were able to move into a part of their convent that was being laboriously repaired.

In 1944, the Germans had to retreat. The Russians took over the country once more. Once more, transports full of forced-laborers were sent off to Siberia. The Terror was even bloodier than four years earlier. The population was decimated. The nuns were chased away again. Five of them were killed on the way or died of starvation.

After three years, the fourteen nuns still remaining asked to be allowed to return. The hospital had in the meantime become a state hospital. They were given permission to return as cleaning women, and moved into the ruins of their convent. Nothing might be repaired or renovated. They tried to make their dwelling draft-free with pieces of cardboard, planks and panes of glass, but it still remained either too hot or too cold or too damp.

For more than twenty years these nuns have been living there under Communist rule. Nine have died. The five survivors still work every day in the hospital. They are paid wages, but the taxes are so high that they have barely enough to live on. They are not permitted to wear their habits. They do their work dressed in rags. They bear their crosses so that they can comfort others by their presence.

Also very heavy is the cross that has to be borne by Christian laymen. As an example we can mention the Hungarian family surnamed Nagy. The family consists of father, mother and four children, of whom the eldest is seventeen. They used to live in

Budapest and had survived the War and the 1956 rebellion without too much damage. They were resigned to their fate, were not members of the Communist Party and went to church every Sunday. Sometimes they were threatened with "measures" to be taken against them, but nothing more serious happened.

A few years later, on Easter Sunday, all the schoolchildren were compelled to take part in a meeting organized by the Party. This is the usual manner of keeping children out of church. The Nagy children arrived late because they had been to Mass with their parents. When the father was called to account for their lateness, he demanded the right to be allowed to bring up his children himself. This boldness determined the fate of the family.

The husband, who had been for years a bookkeeper in a machine factory, was dismissed because he was giving his children an education hostile to the state. He was no longer eligible for work in a state institution. Smaller firms not yet state-owned were already fully staffed or were afraid to employ someone in this situation. Hence that father became unemployed, without benefits. At the end of a fortnight, he had to start selling his furniture and clothing. After three weeks, having no means to feed his family, he volunteered for a "Reconstruction Camp of the Socialist People's Republic of Hungary". Within another fortnight, everything was arranged. The family left for the east. Their few remaining possessions were stored with relatives.

The camp, with a population of about two thousand, consists of a number of concrete huts. In one of these the Nagy family was given a space of twelve by fifteen feet, where they will have to live for two years. Food is distributed three times a day by the communal kitchen. For six days a week they work from eight to ten hours a day. The father and his eldest son are employed in deforestation; the mother works in the laundry. The three younger children are being educated by dedicated Communists. Those who do not go to school have to listen to lectures after their hard day's work, when they are too tired to think. In this way Marxist principles are rammed into their heads.

They are well treated, and the food is acceptable. Only coffee and chocolate are not to be had; and there is a shortage of medicines, winter garments and blankets. Instead of money, everything is paid in goods. In this way, labor is considered the only thing of value, and life in community, an ideal. Wages depend on the family's productivity. In the case of illness—if it is not serious—there is a reduction in the amount of goods received.

The camp is not a prison, and the people can come and go as they will. But the nearest village is seven miles away, and there is no means of transportation except trucks, which do not travel on Sundays. The people are too tired to walk the fourteen miles. Everyone has to be inside by a fixed hour.

Most of the "volunteers" there have the same history as the Nagy family. But there are also priests and nuns who after being released from prison are not allowed to settle anywhere. In order not to starve or to land in prison again, they volunteer for the camp. By a special re-education the government hopes to convert them to Communism. A few "peace priests" have taken this task upon themselves.

After two years, everyone is free to leave the camp. If there are no complaints against them, each one gets a sort of diploma. With this they can always find a position and even a house. Some people leave without a diploma but are then usually back within the week. There are families who have been living in this "reconstruction" camp for six years. The Communist youth organizations often make excursions to these camps. For in these camps are not prisoners but volunteers: voluntary socialist workers in the Reconstruction Camps of the People's Republic! The state is proud of the camps. This is the cross of the contemporary religious persecution in Hungary.

And what must we think of Bishop Tsu-Mang, who died in China? He was one of the very best. Some years ago he reported that the Communists were trying to hypnotize him. In his last letter he wrote: "I beseech you, pray for the Church in China. The future looks very alarming. It is their intention to wrench the Faith out of the hearts of the people and to separate them from the pope." Ten months later he illicitly consecrated a Communist priest and made him a bishop. What had the Communists done to him in those ten months? What did he suffer in that black night when he lost the mastery of his will? There too was a cross on which our brothers had to die.

Another cross is being borne in Lithuania. A Capuchin priest lives there who was for many years a forced-laborer in Siberia. Like Saint Francis, the founder of his Order, he cleans and repairs neglected churches. Then, at night, he recites the Office there and offers up holy Mass in complete solitude. Every time, on account of this, the authorities send him to a new compulsory place of residence. He writes: "I have now been a month in my new place of residence. I am living in a cellar. Providence has once more provided me with an abandoned church that requires a lot of sweeping, cleaning and sprucing up. I thank God that in this way I am able, for a very small part, to carry out the will and testament of our holy Father Francis. The heaviest work has now been done. I am going back now to say matins and shall remain in adoration the whole night. Then I shall be quite alone with God in this deserted church. I am praying for you and for all those who are helping me through your mediation. The Breviary and the books I have received are a great consolation and help me to bear my cross."

Here follows the report of the way of the cross of the Greek-Catholic priest Ghiurghiu Straja. When he was arrested, he was the parish priest of a Romanian mountain village. He was married to Marina, and their little daughter, Tamara, was four years old. It happened in 1948 shortly after the Russians had begun to exploit the uranium fields. At night drunken Russian soldiers used to wander around the farms and rape any women and girls who fell into their hands. In less than two months six women had been murdered. Many women fled to the surrounding villages. Those who remained usually spent the night together in

the attic of the priest's house. The Communists, however, discovered this hiding-place, and one night the women and the
priest were all arrested. Only little Tamara remained behind.
Ghiurghiu was sentenced to prison and never heard anything
more of his wife and little daughter.

In the Aiud prison, Straja was a model of tact and kindness.
By his example, prayers and teaching he converted a group of
Jehovah's Witnesses. His behavior even won the respect of his
guards. The political commissary thought this so dangerous that
he had him transferred to the Jilava prison. In Jilava, Straja swept
the cells every day and did the washing for old and sick people.
By his helpfulness toward everybody he proved that he was a
priest for all. With a number of atheists he discussed the Catholic
faith. Some of them were converted. During an examination by
the camp commander, Stefan, Father Straja was able to convince
him of the existence of God. A few days later Stefan was dismissed and Straja was transferred to the Baia Sprie lead mines.
Before his departure he gave a fellow-prisoner a letter for his
little daughter. As the man was soon to be released from prison,
the priest asked him to search for Tamara and hand her his letter.
She was nowhere to be found, and at long last the letter arrived
in the West. It reads as follows:

Dearest Tamara. Somewhere your father wrote this for
you. My thoughts are always and everywhere with you. I
see your little fair head on every wall and I hear your voice
in the whispering of the rain. If only you still had your
mother, then you would not be an orphan among strangers
like a flower among thorns. Take this letter straight to your
teacher and ask him to tell you everything that I have
written. Ask him to write down all that you know about
Mamma. You must then sign it yourself. Darling, I don't
know when I shall come home. Promise me to tell your
sorrow only to Our Lady and to your dolls. Promise me
to be good and, before you go to sleep, to weave a beautiful
wreath of prayers for your guardian angel.

Ghiurghiu Straja did not survive his transfer to Baia Sprie very long. He was there given the heaviest and most dangerous work. One day he was put in charge of dynamiting. He was buried under the exploded lead ore. For a week the commissary forbade the people to look for his body. The priest had said that God would bury him. In this way Ghiurghiu Straja paid with his life for having defended the women and girls of his parish. His way of the cross lasted for nineteen years.

Near the beginning of 1967, a messenger from the pope traveled to Hanoi. He did not arrive with empty hands, because the Church desires fervently to heal the wounds of war even in North Vietnam. He was officially received by Ho Chi Minh but in spite of his repeated urgent requests was not given permission to visit the archbishop.

How terrible must have been this archbishop's despair on seeing the pictures of this foreign prelate in the newspapers and learning that he had visited Ho Chi Minh and the priests in league with the Communists, while he himself received neither greeting nor any word of comfort from Rome. Did he know that the papal messenger waited near the cathedral for hours but that every attempt he made to reach him was prevented by the panic-terror of those surrounding him? In Hanoi the angel of consolation was driven away from the Mount of Olives. Uncomforted, the archbishop had to go on bearing the cross on which so many have already died.

Finally, one more letter from Bulgaria:

It is cold in my room and I can hardly write without trembling. My hands are not yet used to the blows of the ax, and my heart sometimes rebels against my unbearable lot. I would like to ask you a favor. Tell your friends in the West the story of my life so that they can understand what Communism is.

· Before my country fell under Communist rule, I lived

with my parents and my younger brother. My elder brother was married and had a little daughter. In spite of the fact that I was so young, my bishop appointed me to be a parish priest. Shortly after that the Russians arrived. We were at once put under restraint. We were prohibited from publishing our parish magazine. It was just before Christmas, and I had a lot to say to my parishioners. So I wrote a letter that I did not sign. We made 120 copies, which my two brothers distributed during the night. My share of the "crime" remained secret, but they were caught. Both were sentenced to seven years forced labor. After three years my elder brother was to be pardoned. We got everything ready for his arrival home. Three weeks before he was to be released, we received the news that he had been killed at his work.

From that moment we did everything we possibly could to get my younger brother released. I shall spare you a description of the difficulties. He returned, and that was the chief thing.

In the meantime I was forced to join the army. After five months they discovered I had a heart ailment, and I was dismissed from the army. With my parents I moved to the new parish where I had been appointed parish priest. Everything became much more difficult. My sermons were copied down in shorthand [by Communist officials]. They were looking for a means to strike at me. By means of pamphlets, the people were stirred up against me. The next day the baroque statue of Our Lady lay shattered on the ground before the church door. My brother, with the help of a few friends, put the pieces together again and carried it into the church and adorned it with flowers. A week later my father was arrested. Soon afterward he was taken to the prison hospital. The doctors said he was incurably ill. He suffered terribly.

In the middle of the winter I had to leave my rectory. I had to leave the town at once. Nobody dared to have me

and my mother in the house for longer than one night. At
last we found shelter in a tumble-down summer cottage
in the middle of the woods. It was bitterly cold there, and
the snow penetrated through the cracks in the walls. The
secret police soon discovered us. I was no longer allowed
to function as a priest, as I was dangerous to the state. I
now work in the state forests as a woodcutter. Last week
my mother died. Of my father I have heard nothing more.
My younger brother sometimes sends me some food, although he himself is very poor. What can I still do for my
people who without priests are being subjected, defenseless,
to a cunning form of propaganda? Pray for my poor parishioners, and also for me, that God may give me the strength
to bear my cross to the bitter end.

Behind these reports there is a world of suffering and torture.
Everywhere—in Poland, in Hungary, in Romania, in Czechoslovakia, in Latvia, in China, in Lithuania, in Vietnam, in Bulgaria—everywhere there are crosses on which our brothers are
hanging. Christ is standing with one foot in the dungeons and
the other in the apartment of those like Cardinal Mindszenty.
He is fettered with all those who live in imprisonment. He is
suffering agonies in the sixty-five million brothers-in-the-Faith
behind the Iron Curtain. He is being scourged in the forced
laborers of all the dictatorships. He is wearing a crown of barbed
wire from thousands of concentration camps. And everywhere
in the world he is hanging on the crosses on which our brothers
are dying. It seems necessary for our salvation.

Why are our lives so much easier than those of the countless
numbers in whom the Master is suffering and dying? Why is
your child not taken from you and placed in a state educational
institution because you remain true to your religious convictions?
Why are *you* not deprived of your livelihood if you go to church
on Sundays? Why are *you* not living separated from all those
who are dear to you?

I don't know and you don't know either. It is a mystery. We are no better than the others and yet we are better off. We, the small minority living in peace and prosperity, are treading quite another path to heaven than the overwhelming majority, who are sinking in want, fear, pain and hunger. But I think that all these afflicted people will be everlastingly happy because they are the least of God's little ones, and therefore his favorite children. After a short time of bottomless sorrow, God himself will dry their tears because they have become one with the Man of Sorrows. We who have only a small part of Jesus' Cross to bear are not being so sorely tried in suffering. But God will test us in love for our neighbor. If we do not go with handfuls of kindness and consolation to our brothers who are now being crucified for our sins—if we are miserly with our abundance—if we do not give everything we can spare to the poor and the persecuted—if we do not become far more generous in our relief, of necessity we shall have to fear for our eternal salvation.

CRY OF DISTRESS FROM THE ABANDONED

In the year 1966, I received, from a Communist country, a letter from workers who, starving for spiritual food, listened to the West-European radio. They belong to the growing multitude of disappointed people who have unmasked Communism as deceit and are looking to the West for rescue. They gather around a transistor radio behind locked doors to hear the voice of the Church. They think that Catholicism is flourishing with us in full vigor. They wish to find strength with us to live heroically. They make an appeal to our spiritual wealth and ask us to send them, through the airwaves, the fire of love.

The letter they sent me with great risk was destined for the speakers of Vatican Radio and Radio Free Europe who are in charge of the broadcasts to Eastern Europe. It is a shattering document of the spiritual starvation of our brothers who are being purified in the burning oven of persecution. It is also a humiliating expression of the illusions they cherish about us. The letter reads as follows:

Dear brothers,

These lines are being written in atheistic captivity. They are the cry of distress of your brothers who are condemned to death. For the Church in this country is doomed. And all of us who hunger and thirst after God are doomed to destruction in the wilderness of godlessness. The number of our priests is decreasing steadily. Within ten or twenty years they will all be extinct. How can our young people, growing up without God, ever belong to Christ? How can their souls live without spiritual food? It is enough to make one run one's head against the wall in despair when one sees all this. We have no religious books and no periodicals except the foolish Catholic magazine that plays up to the Communists; it wishes to give the impression that there is no refined terror here but the greatest freedom of religion.

Your broadcasts, to which we listen eagerly, are the only source from which we can get light and inspiration. They can take the place of books and periodicals, sermons and priestly conferences. They can be for many the last plank of rescue. That is why we wish, hopefully, to inform you what we want from you.

Send us over the airwaves the fire of love. Fire that gives courage to the hopeless, makes those who are fatigued fervent, and will ignite us all. Bring unrest to the hearts of the tepid who are being misguided by the atheistic enticement. Fill the inspired with greater enthusiasm. Remain in intimate contact with us who are imprisoned and condemned to death. Live, pray and work with us. Wrestle obstinately for us with Christ and be importunate with him, just as we also continuously besiege him. Feed the fire that you will send us across the Alps, for our souls' sake, with love and sacrifice.

We beseech you, do not act like officers. Be soldiers and stake your lives. Earn for us through your prayers the strength also to give our lives. Lead holy lives and struggle daily for your sanctification. Do all that you can to sanctify us too. For only saints can achieve anything here. Only saints are able to persevere in this darkness to the very last breath.

Choose carefully the news you send to us. Always give preference to what will give us hope and courage. Give us news of heroic deeds that will spur us on to heroism. Strengthen in us the conviction that Catholicism in the wide world is flourishing in its full vigor of life so that we can share in this fullness and find the courage also to be ready for sacrifice. Arouse in us by sweeping examples the consciousness that we too are capable of doing good and that a man who is full of God is able to do supernatural deeds and is even capable of martyrdom. We beseech you, search the whole Catholic world untiringly for such examples. We are convinced that you will find them. For heroism can never be missing from God's Church. Give us examples from the lives of converts, scholars, artists, young Christians, workers and intellectuals. Examples from the lives of present-day saints, which we can continue further in our own lives.

Teach us to pray. Let us admire the ardor and fire of modern prayer in the words with which our Christian contemporaries now address God. Those who are taught to pray are saved! Be untiring in extending the Rosary and continue to teach us how we can better meditate with it. For untold numbers it is the only form of prayer now possible in practice. Incite us to communal prayer. In homes where the occupants pray together, there can be no atheists. Only family prayer can save its members who are no longer able to attend church, even if the prohibition lasts ten years.

Do not sow hatred but teach us to love Christ and our neighbors. Awaken in us a burning love for our Christian and atheistic brothers. Only if you teach us to love our enemies can we be armed against all their attacks and shall we be able to overcome them and bring them back home. Convince us that God exists and that he loves us. Demand of us unfailing loyalty to him, and take a public stand against religious indifference, ignorance, fear and human anxiety. Give to us, who have to live in the mud of atheism, Christian awareness and Christian pride. Free us from inferiority complexes that are systematically being forced on us.

Do not be offended that we do not sign this letter. You yourselves can conclude from the contents whether we are double agents or prisoners risking their lives for the love of souls. Forgive us if we ask too much. We are writing to you, both from an instinct for self-preservation and to save others. We beg for your love, and we love you in Christ, whom we are prepared to defend stubbornly in ourselves and in others. Send us in his name the fire of Love, the great omnipresent Fire. Maranatha! Come, Lord Jesus! Maranatha! Spirit of God, almighty Fire, come!

On reading these high-pitched expectations, I shuddered to think of the day when the full truth about our Christianity will come to light. For things are not well with the Church. Instead of adjusting the preaching of the immutable truths to modern circumstances, as was the intention of Pope John, the contents of Catholic doctrine are being mutilated by a group of headstrong persons. More and more often do we hear of Catholic intellectuals—unfortunately priests too—who deny the divinity of Christ or his Real Presence in the Eucharist, papal infallibility or the absolute authority of the Church in matters of ethics. The Easter miracle of the Resurrection might, in their opinion, quite well be a fairy tale. Prayers of supplication are disapproved of as misdirected faith promoting social injustice. Mary's virginity is being disputed—and so on.

These are alarming symptoms of degenerating faith within the Church. A great many of those who are breaking down the immutable substance of doctrine do, indeed, avoid any open breach with Mother Church but use their Catholic identity to undermine the faith of simple people. Much of what is now taking place under the banner of *aggiornamento* is nothing but an attempt to relativize the dogmas, laws, institutions and traditions of the Church in accordance with the mentality of the world. Much of what is now happening is not reformation but deformation; it is treachery toward Christ and the opposite of conversion, which is the indispensable condition of our salvation.

We have on our shoulders a great responsibility. We have the Gospel, the sacraments and the warning voice of ecclesiastical authority. Thanks to our centuries-long traditions, we know better than others the difference between good and evil. More than others we are obliged to lead immaculate lives, to practice charity, prayer and apostolic zeal. For it could depend on us whether Christ's name shall be blessed or cursed by people and nations who can know him only through our example. The saying "you are the salt of the earth" applies to us all. If the salt has lost its savor, it will be cast away. The same has often happened, and can also happen to us.

In spite of the revolution instituted by the Council, I am deeply alarmed by the storm of latitudinarianism that is ravaging Catholicism. And I am afraid of a Christianity that adjusts God's commandments to human weakness instead of endeavoring daily with a contrite heart to rise up from sin.

Unfortunately, our Christianity is less excellent than our persecuted brothers think. If we continue to abuse our freedom by reconciling the commandments of Christ with the spirit of this world, we shall destroy their very last hope, just as this hope was destroyed in a Czech priest whom I had invited during the "Prague spring" to visit Western Europe for two months. He is a learned and pious man, speaks five languages and had been in prison for twelve years. He visited six countries in order to become acquainted with the Church in the free world. He listened a great deal, read much and said little. But before he returned to his homeland he pronounced the following judgment on us:

> I have been in prison for twelve years for desiring to remain true to the Church of Rome. I have been tortured for not denying the pope. I have lost everything for my Faith. But this Faith gave me peace and security, which made my prison years the happiest of my life. You in the West have lost your peace in God. You have undermined the Faith in such a way that it no longer gives any security. In your freedom you have thrown overboard those things for which we are suffering oppression. The West has disappointed me. I would rather live for another twelve years in a Communist prison than live any longer with you.

This judgment is probably one-sided and too hard in its generalization, but it must make us pause to think. For it interprets the opinion of the important part of the Church which has not been "enlightened" by dubious commentators on the Council but which has been purified in the blood and tears of martyrdom. And the pure in heart see God's truth better than complacent scholars do.

THE CHURCH AS HANDMAID

On my table lie four drab-looking pages, typed to the edge, full of broken German, showing everywhere traces of an Eastern European author and his worn-out typewriter. The document came straight from Hungary. The writer must love the Church very much to risk sending this dangerous letter. With unflinching honesty he hammered onto the paper all his bitterness and fear. It became a dramatic testimony of religious persecution, so clear that the apostolic soul of the witness can be seen through it.

This document, which I can only partially publish, ought to

strike like a fist on the tables of the armchair-scholars who are poisoning public opinion with their unreal reflections on Church and Communism. It is their fault that there is an increasing number of those who have no serious belief in the menace under which the Church is living. They believe that atheism is becoming reconciled to God. Their eyes are tightly closed to the demolition of the Church that is ruthlessly carried on in all Communist states. They explain away the crimes of the atheists, and they mutter about the weaknesses of their own brothers who have been called blessed by Christ because they are persecuted for righteousness' sake. They praise the traitors who surrender Mother Church to the atheists and set them up as examples of modern, model Catholics to the retarded West. They are blind to reality.

As a relentless document of this reality, God has now sent us this letter from Hungary, which in its untranslatable stammering exceeds anything I have ever read about the diabolical character of the Communist revolution against God. However, judge for yourselves!

I am writing these lines before the countenance of God. I am a Hungarian, father of a large family, who has refused to leave his country and is prepared to give his life for the Church. I have serious reasons to believe that the free West has no clear conception of our tragic situation. I fear that in the Catholic Church there are priests and bishops who cannot imagine how deep our humiliation is. And I doubt whether our Hungarian bishops are able to be entirely frank with the Holy See.

In my country there is no freedom of speech and no possibility of writing with the voice of conscience about the distress of the Church. I have learned that the modern problems of the Church are openly being discussed in the West even by laymen in the greatest spirit of freedom. I should like to claim the right that every Catholic in the West enjoys so that the voice of the persecuted Church might be heard before any alien opinion is formed of her problems. The Hungarian Church has become the hand-maid of the Communist state. She is in reality not being governed by the last remainder of the ecclesiastical hierar-chy but by government commissaries and officials ap-pointed by the Ministry of Education who are practically secret-police officials. The episcopal administrative ap-paratus under their control is in fact an executive organ of the atheistic state authorities and carries out Communist policy.

Communist officials dictate appointments, transfers, promotions and punitive measures against the clergy, which, "to prevent worse misfortunes", are carried out by the diocesan authorities. The episcopal ordinariates in Hun-gary have become organs of the state. Pious and zealous priests are being illegally removed from pastoral activity. In personal interviews the ecclesiastical administrators do indeed point out they are acting under compulsion, but those who are being punished unjustly ask themselves with bitterness what good can come to the Church from such slavish submissiveness.

An unfailing way of eliminating priests who do not enjoy the confidence of the atheists is compulsory retirement on pension. Priests in the prime of their lives, especially those with much influence on their colleagues, are obliged to ask for retirement, one after the other, on the diocese's orders.

In this way the Church in Hungary has become the slave and the puppet of the atheists. The state commissaries hold all the strings. The priests have been handed over defense-less to their persecutors.

It would not be honest to push the responsibility for this shameful dependence exclusively on the shoulders of the bishops. Some of them have already long since passed the age at which they can be generally considered capable of bearing this responsibility. Others have been broken in mind and body. They no longer face the problems and are no match for the ruthless collaborators forced on them by the state. Others are just too weak—which is not surprising if you know that Rome can appoint only candidates who are faithful to the regime. The priests surrounding them, who are henchmen and friends of the Communists, bear the most responsibility.

In every episcopal curia there are traitors and opportunists who from fear, greed or thirst for power have accepted their function from Communist hands. Unconditional loyalty to the Church is rarely found among them. No vicar-general or dignitary can be appointed without the approval of the state. All key ecclesiastical positions are therefore occupied by figures who are acceptable to the atheists or who are to be considered even their most devoted friends. With sorrow I must testify that the administration of the dioceses is effectively in the hands of priests without ethics or morals, who have silenced their consciences and have driven the Holy Spirit from their hearts.

I shall cite only two examples: an old and almost senile bishop was forced to accept a vicar-general who is said to have been trained at the Lenin Academy and who never forgets who his masters are; and the secretary of another bishop was greeted during a confirmation tour by a Communist who had taken part with him in a course for secret-police agents.

In the course of the years the atheists have succeeded in getting such a control of the whole ecclesiastical administrative apparatus, by force, blackmail, bribery or treachery, that the bishops who by the grace of the government are still allowed to exercise their functions are quite powerless against them.

The most regrettable role in this development is being played by the so-called "peace priests". Their movement has nothing to do with peace but is an organization trumped up by the government to look after the material well-being of the priests who are members and to ensure

their dependence on the Communist state. It functions as
an exclusive club, sponsored by the state, with a monopoly
on all favors and advantages that the atheistic state can offer
to priests who serve it faithfully.

The whole ecclesiastical administration swarms with
leaders and active members of this dangerous movement.
Among them are individuals striving for money, rank and
titles, psychopaths full of resentment or inferiority complexes, cowardly flatterers of the powers that be, newly
made abbots, provosts and canons. These spiritual *parvenus*
(upstarts), despised by the Christian people, are held up to
us as examples by the government. They behave like
preachers inspired by the Holy Spirit and saviors of the
Church. From their ranks, Rome, according to the will of
the atheists, would have to appoint new bishops; but they
are not good shepherds, being merely hirelings who desert
their flocks and sell their fellow-priests to the Communists.
Before God's countenance and in the presence of the whole
Catholic Church, I consider it my duty to testify that the
Bride of Christ, Queen and Mother of all nations, has
become in our country, not only by honest persecution
but also by the perfidy of a number of her elected sons,
the slave of atheists. This is the true state of the Catholic
Church in Hungary.

This was the letter. Between its lines I see Christ in the desert.
After he had fasted there for forty days, the Tempter arrived
and carried him up onto a mountain and demanded that he
kneel down and worship him. With sovereign contempt the
Master turned his back on this blasphemous presumption. The
Antichrist retired to abide his time. That day has now come.
The essential content of this letter from Hungary consists in
the proof that God's humiliated Church is now being forced
to kneel before the Tempter. Satan is avenging the defeat that
he once suffered against Christ. He is now abusing the chosen
limbs and sacred organs of Christ's Mystical Body for his revolt

against God. Thus the Church has become the handmaid of the devil.

Everything points to the fact that the Communists, with a smile of peaceful coexistence on their lips, desire at all costs to penetrate into the episcopacy, the last stronghold still intact. That is the purpose of their negotiations with the Church, which is like a lamb among wolves and is doing her utmost to lighten the unendurable lot of her children. For this reason alone, conversations with Communist governments are being continued. For the Church, whose highest norm is the commandment to love, cannot indulge in the slamming of doors. This must be done by others. On the other hand, she cannot suffer henchmen of the atheists to mount the bishops' thrones in the glorious Hungary of Cardinal Mindszenty. It would be better to live without officially recognized bishops in the catacombs of illegality than to enjoy a sham freedom in which, behind the façade of well-paid princes of the Church, the life of Christ is being killed in the hearts of her children.

The Church is in peril. That is why we must be on the alert and pray fervently for the conversion of the traitors; for strength for the feeble; for light for the erring; for wisdom for the Vatican diplomats; for God's blessing on the witness who dared to write the letter printed above; and for a flaming sword for the archangel Michael, that he may protect Hungary and by the power of God drive back Satan into hell.

HOLY ILLEGALITY

It was Thursday afternoon, February 27, 1964. The Slovakian village of Likavka was humming with people who had streamed in from the whole neighborhood. On the stroke of three, a funeral procession left the church. The coffin, borne by four workmen through the affected multitude, was covered by a purple chasuble and surrounded by thirty-two small girls dressed in white. Behind the bier followed, praying, the parish priest, two other priests and hundreds of parishioners. Likavka was celebrating on this day both the funeral and the first solemn Mass of an inhabitant of the village, who had been killed by an accident and whose priestly dignity had been concealed from the population for fifteen years.

Only after his death, when the elderly parish priest, with tears in his eyes, produced his best sacerdotal vestments from the sacristy in order to cover the coffin, did the news spread like wildfire that Benjamin, the man who had been killed, a bricklayer, was secretly a priest. The district rose as one man. The night before the funeral the church was too small to contain the number of Christians who kept prayerful watch around the bier.

Father Benjamin had never been able to say Mass in their church. He was one of the unknown heroes who had been ordained without public ceremony, secretly and illegally. No one had known about it. But now there was nothing more to hide; and the few people who knew revealed the secret. They considered themselves obliged to honor publicly the election of the fellow-villager. Thus his funeral became in the midst of this Communist country a manifestation of faith, respect for the priesthood and loyalty to the persecuted Church.

When the seminaries were closed in Czechoslovakia, Benjamin had remained true to his vocation. Released from the concentration camp, he had made his vows secretly. In the evening he had studied under the guidance of a trolley conductor who said his breviary every day at the same hour and in the same church: a dismissed professor of theology whose name is well known in the West.

Benjamin longed for the altar of the Lord, although he would in all probability never be able to say Mass in a church. His aim was a priesthood on the cross without earthly advantages or honor. After he had reached his goal, he never preached a sermon and never taught the catechism. Without recognition, he spent his priesthood as a bricklayer in the midst of his unfortunate people. He consoled the oppressed by nothing more than his presence, his optimism and his encouraging word. He supported the weak and strengthened their hesitating faith. That the testimony of his life was not in vain, his Communist comrades proved when they carried him on their shoulders to the cemetery.

The worker-priest Benjamin was not only in his daily work but also in his suffering and death a brilliant example to all. He had been working with his shift in an almost-finished building. Suddenly a loud explosion was heard, and the whole story was in flames. All the others were saved, but he was the last to jump out of a window—he fell like a burning torch. Burned to the bone, he lived for another week. Those around him were astonished at his patience and unruffled serenity. He suffered unendurable pain. Why did he not complain? How could he possibly open his mutilated mouth to make a joke? The doctors admired him. When afterward they learned that he was a priest, their admiration changed to veneration. Before they were able to amputate his two arms, he went radiantly up to God. For he had fulfilled his vocation and accomplished his priestly mission. He is buried at Likavka, in a Communist country. There are flowers on his grave. He is an example to everybody.

Where church structures are being violently destroyed, God, who is eternally young, is creating new forms of sacerdotal life and heroism. Where the Faith is in deadly peril, it is not sufficient for Christ's servants merely to administer the sacraments. As evidence, God has perhaps permitted that thousands of priests behind the Iron Curtain are never or seldom able to exercise their exalted function. And yet they remain priests to eternity. They must themselves become living symbols through whom God can impart his grace to souls. Is this not our duty, too? The Church will never and nowhere be destroyed as long as her priests give a clear and irresistible testimony of a life that can be lived only through Christ and in God's strength.

Father Benjamin had done that. He had built bridges to God. He had given strength to many. He will inspire numbers of people with a new spirit. The priestly life of this Slovakian laborer, whose first Mass was his own requiem, had borne more fruit in oppression than if it had been spent undisturbed in the service of the Church.

But Father Benjamin would never have become a priest if there had not been a secret hierarchy behind the Iron Curtain, one that has withdrawn in secret illegality into the catacombs—a hierarchy able to face the storm of persecution because it does not depend on vulnerable organizational forms, which, however ancient and venerable they may be, become worthless and even dangerous to life as soon as they are instruments in the hands of God's opponents.

While teenagers in Communist countries are burying their socialist ideals to the accompaniment of American dance rhythms, and while the Soviet system is groaning under tensions for which Communism has no remedy, millions are waiting for the Gospel. Of no use are bishops bound with gold chains to the regime; what is required are apostles purified in the furnace of affliction, who proclaim the Gospel by their lives in the tumult of factories or the silence of their inner rooms. Not the maintenance of organizational structures undermined by Communism, but the imperceptible penetration of God's vital power through the arteries of the Mystical Body—this is a guarantee of the future of the Church, making her into a holy Symbol that in the long run not even Communists can resist.

The Church in Communist countries is living a double life. For practical reasons she is still tolerated temporarily as the official Church, but she is completely under Communist control. She has been banished to the narrow field of liturgical worship, systematically hampered in her preaching, made sterile by the forced limitation of the vocations to the priesthood, and isolated from the oppressed people by the forced collaboration of a number of her higher dignitaries. In spite of open places of worship and decorated "peace priests", the Church is not free. She is doomed to destruction and can rightly be called the "Dying Church".

As she is bound, by reason of her divine principle of life, to develop her own activity, she cannot be satisfied with what atheists deign to allow her. Obeying God rather than men, she is withdrawing to the catacombs, where she is living in holy illegality. What now follows is the story of the flourishing condition and activity of this Church of the catacombs, which was told me by a clandestinely consecrated bishop.

I will begin with one of the hardest blows that the persecuted Church has received: the dissolution of the religious orders and the arrest of all regular clergy and religious. I was then studying theology. At midnight the police forcibly entered the seminary, herded us into buses that were standing ready and transported us to an unknown destination.

At that moment I thought my whole religious future and the priesthood, my life's ideal, lay shattered. It had cost me many sacrifices and was now not far off. After all that we had heard and experienced we did not know whether we were to be killed or exiled to Siberia, but in any case ordination to the priesthood seemed quite out of the question. God reassured me, however, by the words of Scripture: "Did you then not know that the Christ had to suffer all these things in order to enter into his glory?" Like a revelation, the secret of the Cross suddenly shone in new glory: it was a mystery into which, in the concentration camp, we were privileged to penetrate ever deeper.

There were seven hundred of us priests and religious, living in one camp. At first, the priests felt like fish out of water, for they could neither administer the sacraments nor exercise their functions as pastors. But it soon became clear to us that we were only servants of the High Priest, who was offering up his Mass on the Cross of Calvary, by which he has redeemed the world. Thus it came about that we began to understand our true vocation. What in the beginning was for us a hell turned gradually into a paradise. We learned to see that the principal task of the Church does not consist in preaching, teaching, the building of churches and success, but in suffering. For even now the Lord wishes to suffer in his Mystical Body in order to redeem the world.

After I was released from the concentration camp, I looked for an opportunity that would enable me to become ordained. This was not a simple thing, because all the bishops were in prison or in strict custody in their residences. After a long search I at last succeeded in being ordained in a hospital. It took place in a very primitive way.

If I had studied in a normal seminary, the grace of priesthood would have come to me slowly but certainly, almost as if after so many years of study and preparation I had a certain right to it. Now that I was being ordained in—humanly speaking—impossible circumstances, I felt how exceptional and totally undeserved this grace was that I was receiving, almost as if not the bishop but God himself was laying his hands on me.

After my ordination I sent a telegram: "Operation successful, patient can be visited." This was the signal we had arranged to let the other priest-candidates know they might also come. My first task was to organize the ordination of priests in the hospital. Afterward we preferred the open air in the mountains or the privacy of a reliable family. Shortly afterward the secret burden of the function of bishop was also laid on my shoulders. God has always helped me.

It was moving to see the candidates, coming from near and far. They were almost all working men. For all the practicing Catholic intellectuals had been banished to the factories and had time and opportunity enough as workers to prepare themselves for the sacred ordination by private study. When I anointed their calloused hands, I saw in their radiant eyes the willingness to die for God. After the ordination I often said: "Dear brothers, something magnificent has happened to you. You must return to your factories to take up your tools again, but from henceforward your hands are consecrated. They are the hands of priests. Even if you should never mount the steps of an altar, your work will be the work of priests." It was touching to hear married men say: "The Church needs priests. The officially ordained priests are in prison, are prohibited from functioning or are strictly guarded. We are prepared to take their places. We are prepared to live in abstinence. What must we do?"

It is a source of great joy to be allowed to work for God in such circumstances. It is comforting to see how many families are risking persecution and destruction by the government in cooperating with this clandestine apostolate. It is impressive, after holy Mass in the kitchen or attic, to hear a father say: "This is the finest day in the history of our family because Jesus himself was our guest."

One of the more hopeful experiences we have in Eastern Europe is the encouraging certitude that the priesthood of the Church is sufficiently vigorous to break through the usual forms of divine worship in exceptional circumstances and to be present in a world estranged from God in a new fashion. Undoubtedly this is dangerous. Experience has taught that no priest may venture to seek this way of life on his own initiative. Only those who, according to the word of Pope Paul VI, are convinced that the first duty of the priest does not at all lie in being a worker-priest or in carrying on a dialogue, but in centering his sacerdotal life on the divine sacrifice of the Eucharist—only they can count on God's help when the bitter vocation of worker-priesthood falls to them. This truth is illustrated by what is said in the following letter:

I am a worker-priest in Czechoslovakia: one of the hundreds who were forced to defrock themselves because the state considered them unfit for pastoral work. We are no lovers of experiments. We are no pioneers out to discover new forms of apostleship. We bear with difficulty the cross that has been laid upon our shoulders.

Our lives are bare of all romanticism. In the very early morning we say holy Mass in solitude; and in the evening, dead tired, we say our breviary. This is our only foothold. If we lose this we are lost. We are deprived of the spiritual satisfaction that is usually attached to the priesthood. We are not invigorated by the presence of the faithful celebrating the Holy Sacrifice with us. We never baptize a child. We cannot reconcile sinners in confession. We may not speak to young people about God and cannot guide souls on their journey toward sanctity. Thank God that most of us still have our mothers. These are our guardian angels in temptation, which, through loneliness and lack of human success, can sometimes be inhumanly heavy. They share our dwellings and our suffering and accompany us with their prayers. They help us to remain true to the obligations we have voluntarily taken upon ourselves and from which we might with more reason be dispensed than many of our brothers in the West, whose apostasy is so triumphantly held up to us as an example by the Communists. May God help us not to follow this example.

After our mothers, our chief support is books of theology. We borrow them from one another and copy whole chapters—although doing so is punishable as religious propaganda—and we are as happy as children when friends in the West provide us with a few recent editions. These preserve us from mental dullness and insanity, to which the minds of some of us have fallen victim.

In the factories where we work, it soon becomes known that we are priests. Therefore by accepting voluntarily a life in contumely and poverty we are able to refute the atheists' propaganda picturing the priesthood as a profitable "business". Our colleagues are led to reflection, not by our words but by our lives. Many have discovered the living Church after having found in the place where they work a worker-priest whom they have learned to appreciate as a "fine fellow".

Many of us who consider our lives among the workers a grace are now preparing for the future when we will no longer be preaching Christ by silent deeds only, but also in sermons and teaching. The few leisure hours the worker-priests have are devoted to study. They are making great sacrifices in order to be able to follow the theological development introduced by the Council.

One day the Church will need us again. In this diocese there is an average death-rate of twenty priests a year, while only two new priests are ordained. Throughout the whole country the number of priests is diminishing by 12 percent a year. Our parish clergy still functioning as such are, on average, sixty-six years old. It is easy to determine when priests will become extinct here. That is why we pray every day that God may shorten the time of affliction and grant freedom to the Church before we are too old.

The small number of us who in recent years have been allowed to return to pastoral work bring a new relationship toward their colleagues. They are prepared to share their lives and work with others. They know from their own experience that the laity have to sanctify themselves in and through their work and that they can preach Christ emphatically if their whole lives are permeated with the love of Christ. Thus the pastoral work of these colleagues is supported by a new optimism. They are particularly open to the pastoral demands that the Council makes on the priest today.

This is true especially for those priests who come out of prison. Some have used their time with extraordinary self-control, submitting themselves to a strict timetable of prayer, meditation, spiritual training and handcraft, thereby surmounting both boredom and despair. A friend who spent six years in solitary confinement prepared a sermon every morning, although he was never able to deliver one. As a recreation he spent an hour every day thinking out plays. The rest of the time he spent in prayer,

in love for his guards and in sleep. He acquired for himself an inner assurance and a clear spiritual insight that give a special depth to each of his words.

Like him, many worker-priests have found a new relationship toward the Communists once they have tried with heart and soul to love them sincerely. They discovered the triumphal power of love, making brothers of those who despise and torment them. They know that the frequent and mocking question of the Communists as to where the love can be found that the Church has been preaching for two thousand years is really an asking for God. For God is love. No honest Communist can stand up against a confrontation with love. And not infrequently it happens that a Communist secretly returns to God because a worker-priest has silently loved him.

WITH GOD IN RUSSIA

In 1967, I paid another visit to the transit-camp Friedland, where Aid to the Church in Need, especially during the years immediately after World War II, received the refugees and repatriates from East Germany, Poland, Russia and Siberia uninterruptedly, with hands full of love. More than two million four hundred thousand people took their first steps into freedom here. In the next few years, more than five hundred thousand persons from Communist states are still to be expected. Their faces are marked with suffering and hardships. The faces of those who come from the immensity of Russia are especially drab, gray and bloodless. Only their eyes show a sparkle of joy on having regained their freedom.

The chaplain of the camp, Monsignor Wilhelm Scheperjans, who was once a sailor on a submarine, told us about a man of seventy-two who recently came from Siberia. Before refreshing himself after the endless journey, he went to the church to pray. When the chaplain went to fetch him at the end of an hour and a half, the man said: "Father, for twenty years I have not been able to kneel before God's tabernacle. In all that time I have not been able to attend Mass or receive Communion. I never saw a priest. Do you think I could now go to confession and receive Communion? I have been fasting since midnight, even though I am very hungry, because I was looking forward most to Holy Communion. In Russia I prayed a great deal every day, but I missed Mass and Communion more than anything else."

In reports from repatriates from Russia we hear often about inhuman deportations and the tearing-apart of families, and about the innumerable deaths of young people. But how little we know of the inner religious life of our brothers and sisters in the Soviet Union, of their superhuman strength, their loyalty to the Faith, and their brotherly unanimity, which radiates far across the solitude of Siberia and Kazakstan.

Sitting opposite us in the Friedland Caritas House is Frau Böcker* (age seventy-nine) with her daughter Anna (forty-two) and her granddaughter Elfrieda (eleven). They returned the day before from Makalevka in the district of Karaganda. Frau Böcker's husband was deported by the Russians at the beginning of 1945 and died while he was being transported to the Urals. His body was thrown out of the train. Her two sons, Karl and Peter, were at the front. She herself and her four daughters were picked up by the Russians in the neighborhood of Schneidemühl and transported to Russia. After a struggle with the Soviet bureaucracy for some eighteen years, she was given permission to leave the country, but only with her daughter Anna and little Elfrieda. Her son Karl is living in South Germany, and Peter, in America.

But she does not think only of her own children. She feels herself responsible for a whole community of prayerful people in Russia. In spite of her longing to be allowed at last to return to Germany and to see her sons again, it was with a heavy heart

---

*Names and places have been changed to keep from endangering anyone.

that she left Makalevka. "Who will now take over my task there? Who will lead the prayers, baptize the children and bless the marriages?"

Seeing my astonishment, she explains: "The time in Russia was hard and often humanly unbearable, but God was always with us. Every Sunday we had a religious service in the cemetery. There was, of course, no priest and no holy Mass, but the Blessed Sacrament was always in our midst." And then the seventy-nine-year-old woman began to tell extraordinary details about her life with God in Russia.

According to the Soviet laws, it is not forbidden to pray, nor is it prohibited for a larger group of people to gather together in the cemetery. Consequently the Catholics of Makalevka gather every Sunday in the cemetery to pray. A woman named Maria (age fifty-five) is authorized by a priest living a thousand miles away from Makalevka to have the Blessed Sacrament in her safekeeping and to give Holy Communion to the dying after they have said an act of contrition. The priest is able to exercise his functions only clandestinely.

Every month Maria takes the train from Makalevka to the remote city to fetch new consecrated Hosts and to receive instructions. Nothing takes place that the priest does not know about and for which he has not given instructions. Frau Böcker: "We all saved money to pay for Maria's trip to fetch Our Lord. At every meeting Maria carried the Blessed Sacrament in a little bag on her chest. Of the praying members of our community, nobody died without Holy Communion."

On our asking whether the police never took steps against this activity, Frau Böcker replied that the officials very often appeared in the cemetery and had interrogated many people. But nobody ever admitted that Maria had read the priest's sermon or had learned his letter by heart and had communicated it to the faithful. As the agents did not understand German, they were obliged to take as the truth Maria's statement that she had only been reading prayers.

And then Frau Böcker told us of a sad occurrence that took place in 1962. At that time there was a German priest kept prisoner in Makalevka. Every day he did his forced labor, but at night he offered up holy Mass in the presence of faithful Christians, each time in a different building. After he had been doing this for a short time, the police caught him one night saying Mass and maltreated him so badly that he died in the prison weeks later as a result. Since then, there had been no priest in Makalevka. But the police were always afraid of the influence of a priest on the faithful community. So only women were allowed to lead the prayers—without, however, giving a talk.

The old woman told us much more about her apostolate. The priest had not only given her the assignment of leading the prayers at all the meetings but also of baptizing children and afterward to teach them religion. With his authority, she had given the blessing to young couples after the marriage ceremony. All the Catholic mothers in the neighborhood had come to her secretly to have their children baptized. To the betrothed she had given instruction on matrimony and taught them the rights and duties of their state of life. For this purpose she had always received new instructions from the priest through Maria as intermediary. After first having said a prayer of perfect contrition with the marriage candidates and other people present, she had then asked if they wished to marry; and on receiving their affirmative reply, she had declared them bound in holy matrimony. Finally, all those present had kissed the cross as witnesses. She had assisted at no fewer than two hundred marriages and had baptized many more than five hundred children, the last even on the day of her departure.

When we asked her whether she knew of any more such communities of prayer, she replied: "I had no connection with other labor camps, but I am convinced that all the numerous Germans who are still in Russia and have survived the difficult years, pray a great deal. Those who did not hope in God were not able to endure the hard life and intense suffering of all those years. If a person can see no meaning in anything, all that remains to him is despair. Only by God's grace and by prayer can life in the camps of Russia be endured. The Church is not dead in Russia. She is suffering with Christ but she is also living with Christ."

CAIN'S HOUR

Once more Cain has struck his brother down. Sooner than anyone could have expected, the Soviet storm raged over Czechoslovakia. While still in full summer, the "Prague spring" froze to an ice-cold winter in which many illusions as to a more humane Communism, freedom and peace were destroyed.

When in 1968 it became evident that the longing for freedom in Eastern Europe could no longer be suppressed, the Soviet leaders decided to save their situation with Stalinist means. When Prague proclaimed in April a "communist" program in which little or nothing of Marx remained, Moscow declared an implacable war against the rebellious intellectuals. Differences became more glaring. The revocation of countless sentences, the return of those who had been unjustly condemned to the miscarried Marxist society and the human tragedies appearing in their thousands from the documents of the rehabilitation proceedings threatened to hasten the fall of the Red Empire. The revolt of human nature demanding its inalienable rights spread like wildfire. Ineradicable differences of culture and nationality were again discovered. Religious traditions, considered to have been crushed under the steamroller of the dictatorship, flourished anew. The day of liberty seemed to have dawned.

Then the Soviet colossus struck. While the crime was being committed I stood at the border as a powerless observer, witnessing the outrage done to a small and guiltless people.

At the barrier between Berg and Peterzalka, the Czechoslovakian flag flies at half-mast. The customs officials have pasted their customs-house with patriotic slogans and portraits of the arrested Communist leaders, and with manifests in the Russian language intended for the Soviet soldiers. They allow me to pass at my own risk. In the distance, the castle of Bratislava is silhouetted against the clear sky. Closer, at the crossroads to Budapest and Prague, there are Soviet tanks. One of the weary soldiers, who probably has no idea where he is, obstructs the way before me. I ask for an officer and explain to him in German that I am a priest and have undertaken the journey from Rome to visit the sick bishop of Trnava. He shrugs his shoulders and sends me back to Austria. It is half past two. In Bratislava, Danka Kosanova, the seventeen-year-old girl who was shot down on the steps of the university by the occupying troops the day before, is being buried. Now and again I hear the rattle of machine guns. In the evening the radio reports that eighty-four Czechs and Slovaks have already fallen.

I find accommodation in a house full of Czechs and Slovaks who were surprised during their first journey abroad by the sudden end of the Prague dream of liberty. When in the evening they sit before the television screen, sobbing with fury, fear and despair, I can hardly restrain my own tears. The monstrous face of Communism, which, since 1917, has been showing the indelible characteristics of violence, robbery, falsehood and crime, has again appeared, now that the smile of coexistence is no longer opportune. This is one more proof that Communism does not suffer any dogmatic deviations and that it is obliged to suppress all appearances of freedom with all the means in its power. The slogan saying that the Soviet Union is no longer any danger to free Europe has been refuted once more. Communism cannot be liberalized without its ceasing to be Communism.

The Austrian news service with its on-the-scene film pictures is a shattering refutation of Soviet propaganda. Without further ado, the Red Wolf was stripped of its sheep's clothing. Moscow had announced the withdrawal of its troops, but at the same time it had prepared carefully the treacherous attack on a small country that dared to open a discussion as to a system of government forced upon it and that allowed itself an interpretation of Communism in which human freedom is not suppressed.

On the radio I hear the dramatic end of a free transmitter being occupied by the Soviets and silenced: "Here for the last time the voice of the free Slovakian broadcasting station Banska Bystrica. At this moment Soviet troops are occupying our building. We have tried to negotiate with the commander in order to proceed with our broadcasting. But in vain. Dear friends, remain controlled and calm. The truth will overcome." Then followed a hymn, which was broken off in the second stanza. Here, as in Radio Prague, where all broadcasts begin with the first notes of the Hussite hymn "Ye Soldiers of God", the neo-Communists have restored religious values in their opposition to Moscow. Fifty minutes later, Radio Banska Bystrica resumes its broadcast via a secret transmitter.

With the help of an interpreter, I listen for hours to the calls, warnings, reports and directives with which the passive resistance is being organized by numbers of mobile transmitters. This is a miracle of courage, intelligence and organization against which the Soviets, in their feverish attempts to trace these transmitters, are no match.

The television films of the general strike are impressive. The church bells, which for so many years have had to remain silent, now, together with the factory sirens, summon the people to defend their freedom, which even offered the Church a modest viability. The communal distress of these people, who were longing for only a little freedom and were trampled underfoot in a few hours' time as a result, has brought, as never before, unity and unanimity to the country. This is no longer a Communist affair; it is a national rebirth.

It is a heavy blow for the Soviets that numbers of tourists, armed with still and motion-picture cameras, are witnesses to the unimaginable crime that is here being perpetrated. The truth will overcome. The fairy tale that foreign troops have marched into the country at the request of government and Party officials is no longer believed even by the Soviet soldiers. Their morale is suffering noticeably under the total lack of cooperation and sympathy on the part of the population. Passive resistance has given them no peace for five days. The endless discussions with Russian-speaking workers and especially with young people has irritated them and made them uncertain. They have not been out of their uniforms for a single night. Supplies are being held up, so hunger forces them to stop defenseless women and requisition the food they have just bought.

The Soviets have won a Pyrrhic victory that will hasten the fall of the Red Empire. They have shown themselves in their true shape to the world: as an imperialist power keeping its colonial possessions under control by the stationing of troops, according to the methods of the nineteenth century. Never more can the Soviet Union be the center of world Communism. It was the courageous, intelligent people of an industrial state in central Europe who won a moral victory over Moscow. Their human dignity and their national awareness were awakened to new life in the days of open and secret struggle against the occupier.

This new life can no longer be suppressed even by the most barbaric violence. Irresistibly the conviction penetrates the consciousness of numbers of deeply wounded Communists that for twenty years injustice has been done in the name of the ideology in which they have believed. This conviction is being expressed with surprising honesty. It took the Soviets eight months to silence the Communist press in Czechoslovakia and to stop the public confessions in which numbers of Communists have been relieving their consciences.

Not only during the Prague Spring in 1968 but also under the Soviet occupation, Communist newspapers right up to the spring of 1969 continued a shattering denouncement of Communist crimes against humanity, including moral constraint and religious persecution. Our own news service, which had been more and more disputed by progressive Catholics, was thus fully confirmed. In our action for the persecuted Church we acquired Communist allies! One of them was the journalist Milos Vetvicka. In the Czech periodical *Reporter* of February 20, 1969, he published, under the title "Angels among Us", a moving appeal for restitution for the 7,646 surviving nuns and the eleven hundred priests and religious who are, up to the present day, still being treated as pariahs in Czechoslovakia. On account of this article, *Reporter* was banned; but the voice of Milos Vetvicka will no longer be silenced. Here follows his testimony:

They wear long habits and a large cross over the heart. Till quite recently there was a tactful silence in regard to them, except when anything could be said against them. They lived in oppression and discrimination, but they bore their lot with a smile, because they consider Golgotha also a part of their vocation. For they expect no reward here and from us for their generosity and neighborly love, nor for the degradation and torments that they undergo. They hope for Another World, because ours has shown them for years that here there is no justice for them.

There are certain things that we do not know or do not wish to know, or that we forget as soon as possible after we have seen them: one such thing is the world of insanity and hallucinations, the world of deformed children without faces and without limbs, Dante's Inferno, the hell on earth. If you have the courage to penetrate this world you will meet the angels among us, the women in the dark habits and with crosses on their hearts. That is where our society has banished them. I have been in these places of horror, and I shall forget the poor little monsters no more than I shall forget Sister Illuminata and Sister Ambrosia, who are caring for them with love.

Of the original ten thousand nuns, there are 7,646 alive. Of these, about five thousand are employed, and the others live from a scanty pension. They are to be found in Slatinanech or Vidnava, at Javornik or in other places, in Caritas houses, orphanages and other social institutions. Who are the people who have decided the fate of these pariahs? Who gave orders for them to live under the super-intendence of hostile guards? Who refused them the right to be nuns? Who has banished them to ruinous convents in the outer reaches of our country? Who drove them out of the hospitals and the schools? Who banished them from Slovakia to Silesia? Who placed them under moral or physical constraint, made them ridiculous, insulted them and not infrequently had them tortured in dungeons? And why must all these things have been done to them in the name of socialism, which is based on love of one's neighbor and on efforts for a better world?

We can say that the atmosphere of the 'fifties was responsible for all this. But the ones who caused this injustice, the trespassers of the laws, were actual persons! In the night of April 14-15 and again of April 27-28, 1950, transport vans stopped before the convents, and fists began to hammer on the doors. Without further ado the nuns were carried off to their long martyrdom, into the unknown, on the illegal road of outrage and calumny. They were taken under police guard to abandoned convents and interned there as prisoners. Afterward they were forced to work in textile factories, in forests, on state farms, in employment for which they had not been educated at all. They were willing, they worked hard and almost for nothing—always for lower wages than the others. Finally, they were crowded into buildings that had fallen into disrepair in remote areas, without any possibility of contact with parents, relatives or colleagues.

Many of them were unable to endure these hardships and died. Only very few were disloyal to their vows. Most of them to this very day are earning their livelihood at heavy manual labor under inhuman conditions. The most privileged are those working in sanitariums, though always where hell begins—with the insane, with the incurables, with abnormal children. And even there they were till recently underpaid, might not sit for diplomas, might not even follow correspondence courses.

How was and is all this possible? We had our constitution

and some fundamental rights, such as freedom of conscience and freedom of worship. And even in the 'fifties we were decided champions of the General Declaration of the Rights of Man dated December 10, 1948! Article 5: "No one may be subjected to tortures, nor to a cruel, inhuman or degrading treatment or punishment." But ten thousand nuns and two thousand religious priests and brothers were subjected to a brutal and extremely degrading treatment, which was actually not a punishment but in reality an assault upon their human rights. Article 9: "Nobody may be arbitrarily arrested, deprived of freedom or exiled." But the collective action, in the year 1950, against twelve thousand religious persons was totally arbitrary and illegal and was undertaken without any form of trial. Not one of them was officially informed why and how and for how long he was being punished and exiled. Article 18: "Everyone has the right . . . to freedom of worship, as well as to freedom to confess his religion both publicly and privately, alone or in the company of others." It is superfluous to prove that none other than the religious conviction and the communal exercise of religion were the only reasons for these acts of suppression. Apart from a few ridiculous accusations, no one has ever attempted to give a legal foundation to these measures. And even supposing the absurd statement should be true that the nuns of Ostrava were being trained in the use of machine guns in order to carry out a coup d'état—that still does not give anyone the right to generalize and to strike at all, in the spirit of the Middle Ages, when whole groups or nations who maintained a difference of opinion were wiped out.

In the spring of 1968, the religious, too, cherished some hope of reinstatement. In a petition signed by seven thousand conventuals, the Minister of Cultural Affairs was reminded of the hard lot of these outcasts; the celebrated testimony as to the high quality of their work was repeated and the assurance given that they would also in the future be prepared to work loyally "in those places where unity and peaceful coexistence of the human race might need their services". They asked for the repeal of the still-valid administrative measure of 1950 and renounced the restitution of their confiscated property.

I have spoken with many of them, with simple nuns and with their superiors, women of high education and simplicity, who quietly and humbly appeal for justice. And I think that in a state that still proclaims the "January policy" through the mouths of its highest authorities and which has still not said that socialism with a human face is a thing of the past, in this republic each unjustly treated citizen has the right to restitution. If he has no right to it, we should tell him why not—however late (after twenty years) it may be. Or is our society, which is based on the enormous power of the Communist Party, on nationalized industry, on trade unions, on so many other organizations with millions of members, afraid of these eighty-seven hundred members of the moribund religious communities? Were they in their charitable and educative work really enemies of the socialist order? They are asking only for the right to live in poverty and abstinence in the midst of their own colleagues so that they might serve the community and God. There is nothing antisocialist in this service. It is service in hospitals, in charitable and social institutions, in homes for orphans and abnormal children. They wish also to serve the Church by baking hosts and making vestments. Is this antisocialist?

They are not antagonistic toward us. They received me very kindly even though they saw in me, a journalist, a representative of the powers who have done them so much harm. They invited me to their table, and I shared their simple meal. They showed me everything. I took photos of them. Religious, Czechoslovak citizens. All without exception assured me of their love for our country; not one of them uttered a word of criticism against our social order.

In spite of the wrong that has been done to them and of which I can only write with shame, there is no trace of hatred. On my repeatedly asking about this, I received always the same answer: We forgive everyone who has done us harm and we pray for them in accordance with the Gospel. In the Caritas house at Javornik, I enquired about their political interest. The superior assured me: "Yesterday we heard Mr. Dubček over the radio. We are praying for him." And when I asked for their opinion of Jan Palač, a nun whom I met in Prague declared: "Suicide is always terrible, but we sympathize with this martyr and are praying for him. And not only for him but also for all our compatriots and for our homeland."

With downcast eyes, in her dark habit, the nun went her way. She took no notice of the crowd. The children gazed after her as if a ghost had passed, a shape from the world of yesterday. But before my mind's eye I saw the hundreds of simple, industrious women who have forsaken all the joys of the world, given up all possessions, in order to serve others who are in the greatest need. I remembered how contemptuously they had been treated and how they had been exploited, how after a whole lifetime of toil they had two hundred kroner thrown at them by way of pension, which was not even enough to maintain them in the poor-houses of Caritas, so that the younger nuns, whose annual wages had been fixed by the authorities at six hundred kroner, had to help support them. All this came into my mind. Also, the eyes of a mute and paralyzed little human being in one of the institutions where no lay nurse will ever agree to work. They were the eyes of a sixteen-year-old boy whom the nun had taught—how, I don't know—that sixteen years of suffering on earth were worth an eternal reward in heaven. I saw the eyes of these afflicted children when the sister stroked their misshapen foreheads with her white hand. That is why I wish to be the advocate of these eighty-seven hundred Czechoslovak pariahs. It

should be self-evident to everyone that they must be restored and recompensed.

The restitution of those pariahs has no more taken place than
the reinstatement of the Archbishop of Prague, Jozef Beran.
After nineteen years in captivity, he was made cardinal in 1965
and received the government's permission to travel to Rome.
He was convinced that he would return to Prague. When his
return was made impossible for him, he lived for another four
years in exile, cherishing to his very last day the hope that he
would be allowed to die in Prague.

The dramatic events in his homeland gave him, in January
1969, one more cause to show his pastoral care. After the
death of Jan Palač, he spoke to his afflicted people via Vatican
Radio:

> This is a sad and great hour. Listen once more to my voice,
> which is full of grief and love. It is the voice of your old
> archbishop of Prague, Cardinal Jozef Beran, speaking to
> you from Rome. At this moment it is, alas, impossible for
> me to come and see you after so many years of absence,
> although that is my most fervent wish. But my heart is
> with you. As shepherd and citizen of this dear and blessed
> land, I take my share of the suffering with which it is now
> afflicted and hope that it may become a greater and more
> united land in sorrow and in hope.
>
> I weep with you for the tragic death of Jan Palač and of
> the others who have followed him. I admire their heroism,
> even though I cannot approve of their despairing deed.
> Suicide is never human. Let no one repeat this deed, but
> may it remain in the memory of all, so that all may live
> for the ideal for which they have so cruelly sacrificed their
> young lives. He who speaks to you has suffered much, as
> you know. But the time has come to forget the past. Let
> us not waste our spiritual strengths in hatred: but let us
> dedicate them once more to unity, to labor in the service
> of our brothers, to the new growth of our country. Let us

be a good and strong people. Let us open to our young people the road to hope.

You ask me how I can speak in this way, being so far away from you. I give you my answer: I can because I must. In Christ I am your teacher, your guide, your friend, your father. And I must because I believe. My Faith is my light. My hands raise up this light for you, to call you, to guide you, to greet you. If this should be my last effort of faith and love for you, if it should not be given me to see you again, consider this my spiritual testament. Do not reject it. Do not forget it. *Sursum corda*, children and brothers! *Sursum corda*: may your strength be in silence and hope.

On May 17, 1969, he died in Rome. We had known him very well. He was a good and peace-loving man. It was sufficient to meet him to appreciate how inhuman and devilish the system must be that tormented and persecuted him for twenty years and till the hour of his death. We bow our heads in reverence for his memory, and we repeat at his grave the words that Pope John sent to his prison (via indirect channels) on the occasion of the fiftieth anniversary of his priesthood:

We should like to visit you! It is a source of sorrow to us not to be able to celebrate the anniversary of your priesthood with you. It is not granted to us to address you personally and not even to send you these words of comfort and encouragement by direct means. In spite of everything, you must continue to think that you have done well. You were cast down not for your fault but because of your virtue. The silence and the undeserved punishment imposed on you by injustice will not be fruitless. From the grain of corn dying in the earth shoots a stem that will bear a golden harvest.

FORGIVE US OUR TRESPASSES

Some years ago our ministry was attacked by a Catholic professor as being an alarming phenomenon, an originally realistic and purely religious movement that now is going in quite the wrong direction. He blamed our efforts for having appallingly degenerated. He accused us of un-Christian behavior because in our publications we are doing exactly what Christians ought not to do (sowing fear and hatred); and because we do not do what Christians ought to do (teach the people to understand the positive as well as the negative qualities of Communism and the negative as well as the positive sides of the Western world). After a rejoinder on my part, the professor admitted: "You may publish everything about the religious persecution only if you give at the same time a picture of what the Church had done to deserve the persecution."

As regards this question of guilt, I have had the following considerations: Jesus hides himself by preference in poor and weak people whom he has called the "least of my little ones". If we consider it our task to console him and help him, there where he is weeping, because he is again being hated, persecuted, imprisoned, tortured and crucified, we already know beforehand that Jesus is now no longer suffering and dying in the unrepeatable and for all creatures inimitable perfection of his own sacred humanity, but in the faulty humanity of those who though incorporated in him by baptism yet live sinful lives.

The Church on earth is not only the communion of saints but equally the Church of sinners. All human suffering—except that of Christ—will therefore be burdened with some measure of guilt. And it will never be difficult, with a history book in hand, to show in retrospect that a religious persecution was directed against a Church consisting of imperfect popes, bishops, priests and faithful.

But it is really going too far and is not Christian to demand on these grounds that we tactfully refrain from speaking of religious persecution without carefully measuring out the degree to which the persecuted are themselves to blame for their fate.

It is nowhere written in the Gospel that we must increase the suffering of the afflicted by covering them with reproaches. Nowhere is it written that we are obliged to judge our brothers. It is not noble to cast stones from a safe distance at people in distress. If there is any question of blame, then let it never be in respect to others whom we cannot and may not judge, but only for our own guilt and responsibility.

Hence it should be remarked that God has already emphatically said in the Old Testament that we are not responsible for the sins and omissions of our fathers. Neither the Church of today nor we personally are to blame for the rise of Communism. But we are responsible for its continued existence or its disappearance. That is why in Fatima, God's holy Mother made the problem of Russia a matter of conscience for each of us. According to the assertion she expressed in 1917, which is still the only true assertion, world peace depends on the conversion of Russia. And Russia's conversion depends on ours. Our guilt therefore is not in the historical ballast of the past but in our un-Christian behavior of today.

The revelation of Fatima, which, for that matter, was only a contemporary repetition of purely Gospel truths, teaches us that the root of all evil lies not in political, economic or social abuses but in our own hearts. Therefore a spiritual rebirth is the unavoidable condition for every social *and* political improvement. As long as there is no renewal in the hearts and souls of the people, the threat of a third world war will remain.

At Fatima, the Holy Virgin revealed the last remedy against this threat. She did this in the very months of 1917 in which Lenin was preparing his October Revolution, when Communism had not yet come to power and no living person knew what danger was threatening the world. Lenin's revolution, for which no doubt many Christians are equally responsible, was in its essence a total revolt against God; and that has remained the case. It can be compared only with the revolt of Lucifer.

Our Lady's revelation as to how this revolt can be averted and peace restored was believed by very few. The Second World War broke out therefore just as she had prophesied. This war ended in a victory for Communism, which conquered a third part of the world. Millions of refugees and oppressed people, an Iron Curtain straight across Europe, a wall through Berlin and an unprecedented persecution of the Church were the consequences. As a response to the distress that follows Communism everywhere like a shadow, our relief effort was then called into existence to help the persecuted Church.

Our efforts are being opposed by those who believe that God's Church can live in peace with Communism. By saying that Communism has lost its militantly atheistic character, they do harm to our relief work, which interferes with their dialogue with the persecutors of religion. Communism, which Pope Paul VI called "incurable", changes its tactics but never its Satanic purpose: the negation of God, his expulsion violently from the minds, hearts and consciousness of the faithful and the destruction of all religion. The present-day religious persecution in the Eastern European satellite states is therefore by no means an indignant resistance of downtrodden peoples against a Church that has betrayed her mission. It is not caused by the otherwise regrettable shortcomings of the Church in those countries, but by the intrinsic wickedness of atheistic materialism, which denies God in principle and combats him by definition. Therefore no Communist can make his peace with God without ceasing to be a Communist, so that atheistic humanism is valueless for the "world of true men, which cannot exist without God's sun on the horizon" (Pope Paul VI). Peaceful coexistence and dialogues, diplomatic contacts, negotiations and agreements can change nothing in this. Thus Pope Paul VI at Fatima speaks just as clearly as Pius XI, Pius XII and John XXIII of "countries where freedom of worship is suppressed and where the denial of God is forced on the people as the truth of the new times and as a liberation, although this is entirely false".

The journey to Fatima undertaken by Pope Paul on May 13, 1967, in spite of the objections of Catholic priests, intellectuals and journalists, to pray like any humble pilgrim for peace in the Church and in the world, for the Communist countries and their unfree populations, was an utmost attempt to open the hearts of the people at last to Mary's terrible though not-quite-hope-quenching words. Even without removing the veil covering a part of Mary's prophetic message, Paul VI confirmed that there is no other means of escape than obedience to Mary's appeal to prayer and repentance, to which she added—three months before the revolution of October 1917—"If my words are listened to, Russia will be converted; if not, it will spread its errors throughout the world and unchain wars and religious persecution. Many righteous people will be martyred, the Holy Father will have much to suffer, whole nations will be destroyed."

The catastrophes that lie behind us and those with which we are threatened are evidence of the credibility of this revelation, acknowledged by four popes. Nobody is obliged to share this point of view, but in the name of toleration and charity we would beg that enlightened minds in the Church should cease from insulting the Pope and innumerable Christians who stand at his side, cease from wounding them and ridiculing them for the sake of Fatima.

Like a passionate cry of distress multiplied a millionfold by radio and television, the words of Christ's representative on earth, on May 13, 1967, rang over the heads of the pilgrims: "The world is in danger." Is not this danger the more terrifying now that in many Church provinces the salt of the earth is becoming more and more without flavor, and the inner peace and unity of the Church—for which the Pope prayed at Fatima with such emotion—are suffering more and more violence?

Not without reason did the Holy Father repeat—tactfully and in conditional form—his warnings, all too frequently ignored, against spiritual anarchy, which is now threatening the Church. Not without reason did he defend the Christian renewal intended by the Council against arbitrary interpretations, against agitators, against destroyers of the essential ecclesiastical structure, against all those who, instead of exerting themselves with apostolic love for the salvation of souls, are seeking a compromise with foolish modern ideologies and with the profane spirit of this world.

Can it not be partly explained by the ever-deepening spiritual and moral decay in the postconciliar Church, that the danger threatening humanity has taken on such apocalyptic dimensions? Where is the salt of the earth? Where is the light of the world? If this light is quenched by God's own children, is it not inevitable that morally underdeveloped scientists will tomorrow make misuse of their terrible possibilities for murder and destruction? The Pope: "In a world full of the terrible implements of murder, the moral progress of humanity has not kept equal pace with the technical and scientific progress it is making." And he concludes: "The immeasurable and dramatic image of world events is visible here [at Fatima]. The world image revealed by our Lady. The image to which our eyes are turned with horror but still with hope. The image that we shall keep continually before our mind's eye while obeying the commandment—we promise this—to prayer and penance that Mary herself has given us here."

By these last words Paul VI publicly made the vow to pray the Rosary daily and to do penance. He did this for peace. It is an ominous sign that a prominent Catholic daily announced the Pope's pilgrimage under the heading "To Our Lady of the Cold War". Here the devil is sowing confusion in a Catholic disguise. Here the wolf in sheep's clothing has penetrated the fold of God's Church. Those wishing to remain faithful should turn from these traitors and follow the Pope.

All hope is not lost. Miracles still happen. Maybe the fact that young people behind the Iron Curtain are turning away from Marxism is owing to the Rosary prayed by the humble in heart and by their exercise of penance, which is being systematically ridiculed. Is this the prelude to the rediscovery of God? The conversion and baptism of Svetlana Stalin in the headquarters of atheism are symptoms! At the horizon the hope is dawning that

Mary's promise—"eventually my Immaculate Heart will triumph"—will come true sooner than we expect.

The prideful opposition to the role allotted to Mary in God's plan we can break down only by humbly begging for her help. This thought is neither behind the times nor against the true ecclesiastical renewal. I refer to Cardinal Suenens: "Concealed by the activity and intrigues of those prominent in the foreground, a gigantic struggle is taking place; it is the struggle between angels and devils for the salvation or destruction of mankind. The leader of the hellish spirits is Satan. At the head of the celestial hosts stands the Queen of the Angels, whose standard-bearer is Saint Michael. He who has said No to God has entered the lists against the one who has said Yes. That is the true sense of the events of the present times and the only philosophy of history explaining the last causes."

Because we Christians should know this better than all others, we are more responsible than the others for the present state of world affairs. The world will not change as long as we remain the same. We must come finally to the conclusion that two world wars in thirty years' time are an expression of God's annihilating judgment on the life we are leading. The world is under God's judgment, and only penance can help. This is the message of God's roaring voice denouncing us in the abominable fireworks of the atomic explosions.

Communism is terrifying not because it opposes God, but because we forget God; not because it is strong in hatred, but because we are weak in love; not because it kills Christians, but because we do not live like Christians.

In this sense the persecuted Church in the East, which was purified in blood and tears, is much more innocent than the unpersecuted Church in the West. We are still bound by a thousand chains to this earth. We do not persecute Christ but we compromise him. As long as we darken Christ's glory by sin, materialism and selfishness, we shall lack the strength to draw Communists to him, who desires so fervently to rule their searching hearts.

Certainly, it is our fault that Communism continues to exist. That is why, since the Hungarian revolt of 1956, we have held no sermon without a passionate appeal for penance, reform of life and conversion. That is why with regard to the fall of Communism we have never had any expectations of the violent means of this world and have set our trust only in God, in the Holy Virgin and in persevering prayer. That is why we are working feverishly for a better future by giving all imaginable help to the formation of a holy team of those united in God, who, with Jesus in their midst, are to hold a real dialogue with Moscow, the dialogue of the merciful, all-understanding, all-forgiving Christ with the lost lamb and the prodigal son. The words of this dialogue cannot be learned from books but only from the Holy Spirit. Before the dialogue, however, must come our conversion; and only then will God forgive us our trespasses.

The changing of the guard in Red Square, 1947.

Maria Radna, Romania.

Romanian priest ministering to his people.

Memorial to "The Unknown Comrade" above the city of Korce, Albania.

Despite persecutions, people remain strong in faith.

"Let the little children come to me; do not stop them; for it is to such as these that the kingdom of God belongs." (Mk 10:14–15)

Children of Moscow.

Conclusion

LETTER TO CHRIST

Lord Jesus Christ, many years ago I took the liberty of writing you a letter. There being no postal service to heaven, I was obliged to address it to people in whose hearts you dwell. I thank you once more for the favorable response you then gave to my letter.

And now I am standing and knocking at your door. I call to all the windows of your house and ask. For you have again led me into difficulties with your marvelous statement: "Whatsoever you do to the least of my little ones, you have done unto me." I understand this literally. That is why I dare not send away unassisted anyone who asks for help in your name. For I always think that you yourself are standing before me, beseeching, and that you yourself write the letters appealing for my help. That is why I always say yes every time you come to ask for something for yourself.

This has gone well for more than forty years, and you have never let me down. Again and again you have moved the hearts of friends and benefactors so that my hands were filled once more and I was able to accomplish all those things that I had promised in Eastern Europe, Asia, Africa and Latin America for your sake. Indeed, Lord, although I have made a vow of poverty and have renounced all possessions, you have given me the joy of distributing more than six hundred million dollars to people in whom you are suffering. But now you have come to me a little too often.

247

Now you have become too extravagant in your demands. All too obstinately you have followed me with the complaints of your mendicant mouth. Now I am afraid that you have made me promise more than I can perform. For the serious crisis afflicting the Church has also brought confusion and disloyalty to the ranks of my friends. Benefactors who have helped me in the past are now estranged. Others have become tired of always being reminded of the needs of the persecuted. Many have become cool in love or have become attached to the things of this world. To fill the measure to overflowing is the fact that the press, the radio and the television, which in earlier years often sent my appeals in a million echoes around the world, now mostly ignore my cares and suppress my voice, seeing that my action has not the sympathy of those who rule these means of mass communication in a too-dictatorial manner.

You knew all this when you were begging of me so immoderately. But I did not know. And I granted all your requests without taking into account the reverses that will force me to cut down drastically the subsidies if you do not help. You know, Lord, that I am a weak and limited person. You know that I sometimes cannot sleep when I am hectically looking for new means to relieve the distress that you have entrusted to me. You know that I have toiled for you to the utmost limits of my power and that I am now at the end of my resources. Please examine, yourself, our ledger books and the long list of promises that I cannot fulfill. Please calculate, yourself, how many millions you have asked too much and by how many millions I have exceeded my trust in you. And then tell me what I must do.

During recent years you have over and over again asked me for about two and a half million dollars to finance pastoral work among the refugees. Which of the chaplains must I disappoint? If I abandon the help to the Ethiopian, Vietnamese and Czech refugees, I can save three hundred and sixty thousand dollars. Is that what you wish? Then, the budget for the persecuted Church amounts every year to about eighteen million dollars. If I send no motor vehicles to the priests in Eastern Europe this year, I can save six hundred eighty thousand dollars. Is that your wish? And you ask me every year for one million dollars for the training of priests in Poland. They are young people who cannot continue their studies without our support. They are diligent and generous. They are counting on us. If I cancel fifty scholarships, I shall save two hundred thousand dollars, but I shall destroy the future of fifty people. Do you really desire that? And what must I do with the menaced Church in Latin America, Asia and Africa, for which I have had to spend, at your request, since 1962, twenty-six million dollars already?

Do you remember, Lord, how, in need of help, you came to meet me in the person of Sister Rosemarie, in the refugees for whom there was no room in the inn, in so many mothers of sorrow, in Annie Wong in Hong Kong, in the bronze-colored girls of Bombay, in the rugged gatekeeper of Red China and little Wu, in the pig-priest of Cheju, in Precious Pearl at Saigon, in Benito Sakay, who tattooed your weeping face on his belly, in Father Lagerwey in the Philippines, and in Maria Thoi, who brought her child into the world one Christmas night in the camp of Nam Hai? Do they no longer need my support? To which of them must I henceforth refuse help?

And do you remember Father Celsus in the neighborhood of Bacabal, who was traveling around between his two churches and the eighty-three chapels to give spiritual help to the forsaken people? Are you sorry that you interceded for him? Do you also regret that I recognized you in Monsignor Expedito, who is devoting his last efforts to the Church in northeast Brazil, in the nuns of Nisia Floresta, in the deacons on the island of Itaparica, in the weeping widow of Severino Silva, in Father van der Rest, in the wise and courageous cardinals of Salvador and Santiago, in Miguel de Sousa Mendes and his ten children in the favela at Rio? Are they no longer the least of your brothers, and is what I do to them no longer done to you?

Are you no longer alive in the children of the "blond death", in the mud-dwellers of Bukavu and in the poverty-stricken nuns of Mother Hadewych's Priory of the Resurrection? And are you

no longer weeping in the innocent little children behind the Iron
Curtain, to whom belongs the kingdom of heaven, and who are
forbidden to come to you? Must I care no more for the priests
suffering the fate of Joan Tautu, for the nuns in Latvia, for those
in the Ukraine, in Hungary, in Czechoslovakia, in Vietnam and
other places who are prevented from following their vocation?
Have you no further interest in the young workers listening on
their transistor radios to Vatican Radio, Radio Free Europe and
Radio Veritas, and for the Hungarian layman who no longer
understands Vatican diplomacy? Must I do nothing more for the
priest who left us in disappointment and who would prefer to
live another twelve years in a Communist prison than stay one
day longer with us? Do you wish me to leave the clandestine
bishops and worker-priests in the lurch, those who are building
the Church of the catacombs in holy illegality? Do you wish me
to ignore the plight of the Christians living alone with you in
Russia, or that of our downcast brothers in Czechoslovakia who,
following the Prague Spring with its first exhilirating sense of
freedom, have lost all hope? Do you desire that I abandon even
one of all those people who are relying on our help and are
depending on us?

No, Lord, that is not your desire. For you cannot contradict
yourself. After having come to me a thousand times in the shape
of desperate people in need, people who have moved me to make
these promises, you cannot wish me to forsake them now. That
is why I stand at your door and knock. That is why I call to all
the windows of your house and ask. You have said: "Ask and
you shall receive, knock and it shall be opened unto you."

Now therefore move the hearts of all those who read this
book. Let them understand how horrible it will be to disappoint
thousands of poor brethren. Let them honestly compare other
people's want with their own abundance. And let them be merciful to the limit of their power, that they themselves may win
your mercy. Amen.

Contributions can be sent to:

In the United States
Aid to the Church in Need, P.O. Box 576, Deer Park, NY 11729-0576

In Canada
Aide à l'Eglise en Détresse, C.P. 250 (1427 Graham Blvd.),
Montreal QC Canada H3P 3C5

In Australia
Aid to the Church in Need, P.O. Box 11, Eastwood N.S.W. 2122

In Great Britain
Aid to the Church in Need, 124 Carshalton Road, Sutton, Surrey SM1 4RL

In Ireland
Aid to the Church in Need, Holy Trinity Abbey, Kilnacrott,
Ballyjamesduff, Co. Cavan